The Rabbit Handbook

Karen Gendron

**With Full-color Photographs
Drawings by Michele Earle-Bridges**

BARRON'S

About the Author

Dr. Karen Gendron is a veterinarian practicing in New England. She received her Bachelor's degree from Cornell University and her veterinary degree from Tufts University. Her practice is currently limited to small animals including dogs, cats, ferrets, rodents and, or course, rabbits. In addition to veterinary practice, Dr. Gendron hosts a weekly call-in pet show, The Vet Line, on WESX radio in Salem, Massachusetts. She owned her first rabbit while in college, a big old white lab rabbit named Casper.

Photo Credits

Norvia Behling: pages v, vi, viii, 5, 11, 13, 16, 18, 20, 24, 31, 37, 40, 51, 62, 66, 71, 77, 85, 88, 95, 97, 104, 105, 107, 110, 113, 115, 118, 127; Zig Leszczynski: pages 80, 92, 122; Monika Wegler: page 27.

Cover Photos

Front cover: Norvia Behling, Zig Leszczynski; Inside front cover: Norvia Behling; Inside back cover: Norvia Behling; Back cover: Norvia Behling.

All inquiries should be addressed to:
Barron's Educational Series, Inc.
250 Wireless Boulevard
Hauppauge, New York 11788
http://www.barronseduc.com

International Standard Book No. 0-7641-1246-5

Library of Congress Catalog Card No. 99-045789

Library of Congress Cataloging-in-Publication Data
Gendron, Karen.
   The rabbit handbook : purchase, care, and breeding, understanding rabbit behavior / Karen Gendron ; drawings by Michele Earle-Bridges.
      p.   cm.
   Includes bibliographical references (p.   ).
   ISBN 0-7641-1246-5
   1. Rabbits. I. Earle-Bridges, Michele. II. Title.
SF453.G36   2000
636.9'22—dc21
                                        99-045789
                                        CIP

Printed in China

19 18 17 16 15 14 13 12 11

Important Note

This book deals with the keeping and care of rabbits as pets. In working with these animals, you may occasionally sustain minor scratches or bites. Have such wounds treated by a doctor at once.

As a result of unhygienic living conditions, rabbits can have mites and other external parasites, some of which can be transmitted to humans or to pet animals, including cats and dogs. Have the infested rabbit treated by a veterinarian at once (see page 48), and go to the doctor yourself at the slightest suspicion that you may be harboring one of these pests.

Rabbits must be watched very carefully during the necessary and regular exercise periods in the house. To avoid life-threatening accidents, be particularly careful that your pet does not gnaw on any electrical wires.

Contents

Preface   vii

1. **About Rabbits**   1
   History   1
   Description   2
   Life Expectancy   3
   Rabbit Warrens   3
   Rabbits and Easter   3
   Rabbits and Dog Racing   3
   Rabbit Overpopulation   4
   Rabbit Underpopulation   6
   Rabbit Uses   8
   Jackalope—Fact or Fiction?   9

2. **Selecting a Pet Rabbit**   10
   Do Rabbits Make Good Pets?   10
   Is a Rabbit Right for You?   10
   Finding the Right Rabbit   12
   What to Consider Before Buying a Rabbit   15
   Bringing a Rabbit Home   17

3. **Caring for Your Rabbit**   21
   Handling   21
   Rabbit-proofing Your Home   22
   Rabbit Cages   23
   Rabbit Hutches   26
   Caring for Outdoor Rabbits   27
   Ventilation in a Rabbit House   28
   Warm Weather   28
   Litter Box Training   29
   Grooming   30
   Traveling   34
   Tattoos for Identification   39

4. Nutrition   41
Rabbit Physiology   41
General Feeding Guidelines   42
Pellet Feeding   43
Dietary Adjustments   46

5. Medical Care   47
Taking Your Rabbit to the Veterinarian   48
Pain   49
Emergencies   49
Medicating Your Rabbit   50
Specific Medical Problems   53

6. Rabbit Behavior   75
Rabbits in the Wild   75
Digging   75
Vocalizations   76
Body Talk   76
Coprophagy   79

7. Breeding Rabbits   81
Determining the Sex of Your Rabbit   81
Spaying and Neutering/Castrating   82
Sexual Maturity   83
Breeding   84
Kindling   85
The Kits   86
Future Pregnancies   87
Newborns and Orphans   87
Genetics   91

8. Showing Rabbits   94
The ARBA Standards   94
ARBA Registration   94
The Shows   96

9. Rabbit Breeds   98
Colors   98
List of Breeds   101
The Breeds   102

10. **Loss of a Pet Rabbit** 121
    Grieving 121
    Euthanasia 123
    A Practical Note 123

Glossary 124

Appendix 130

Useful Addresses and Literature 131

Index 133

Preface

Who can get through spring without enjoying the wild rabbits they happen across? Every spring, I keep watch for the new, young rabbits who venture into my backyard from their warm dens. For those of you who have rabbits as pets, you also know the special joy of sharing your daily life with a rabbit. Rabbits, both domestic and wild, have had a special place in our lives for ages.

My experience with rabbits has come as much from treating their problems as it has from enjoying them as pets. This handbook has been designed to answer all of your questions about raising and owning a rabbit as well as to help you deal with any medical problems that may arise.

For the first-time rabbit owner, getting things right may seem a little overwhelming. In truth, rabbits are pretty easy to care for. And, you soon discover, rabbits are tremendously personable. Those who think of rabbits as quiet cage pets may be very much surprised.

If you already own a rabbit or several, this handbook will prove to be a great resource for you as well. This is a thorough reference for medical problems and should be used to double-check that you are following an optimum diet. You might also pick up some ideas to entertain your charges.

Always remember that you have taken on the responsibility of caring for a living being. Your rabbit deserves the best.

A Note About Pronouns

Many rabbit lovers (including this one) feel that the neuter pronoun "it" is not appropriate when applied to our furry friends. Therefore, in this book, to avoid the clumsy use of "he or she" when referring to rabbits, we've chosen to stick with the masculine "he" when speaking in general terms. This was a simple editorial decision, and in keeping with Barron's goal to avoid sexist language, no sexism was intended.

The Netherland Dwarf rabbit.

Chapter One

About Rabbits

History

Wild rabbits from Europe and Africa have given us the pet rabbit that we know today. People began domesticating rabbits in the Middle Ages. They are known to have been in the United States as early as the beginning of the 1700s. The Angora is one breed that is known to have been here during that early time. By the 1800s, the Polish and early Dutch breeds were in the United States as well. In the twentieth century, the 1950s brought an expansion in the number of breeds in the United States and growth has continued since that time.

Rabbits are crepuscular, meaning that they are most active at dawn and dusk; they sleep more during the day and at night. As a result, it will be most natural for your rabbit to eat at these times. Your rabbit will also want to play and exercise more at dawn and dusk.

Rabbits have a very light, fragile skeleton. Because of that, we have to take special precautions to make

The Eastern Cottontail is one of the most common rabbits found in the United States.

sure they do not become injured, especially when they are handled.

Lagomorphs

Rabbits, along with pikas and hares, are lagomorphs. Lagomorphs are mammals that are similar to rodents, but rabbits have a second set of upper incisors that rodents do not have. This second set of incisors helps wear down the bottom incisors as they grow. Of course, to look at a rabbit and a rat, you would certainly see many more differences. However, the teeth are the major feature that put lagomorphs in their own group. The scientific name of the rabbit is *Oryctolagus cuniculus.*

Hares are slightly different from rabbits. For example, rabbits are born without any hair, with their eyes closed, and quite helpless; hares are born with fur and with their eyes open. Despite their differences, hares and rabbits can interbreed, but wild rabbits and hares would not make good pets.

Types of Rabbits and Hares

Rabbits and hares commonly found in the United States include the cottontail, the snowshoe rabbit, the jackrabbit and, of course, the domestic, or pet, rabbit. The cottontail is a good swimmer that can escape from predators by running into streams or lakes. It nests on the surface of the ground rather than digging burrows. The snowshoe rabbit is a hare that is not strictly herbivorous (plant eating). The snowshoe will eat mice and the meat of dead animals. It develops so rapidly that it is able to hop by the third day of life. The jackrabbit, a hare, is the fastest of all the rabbits and hares, racing up to 45 mph (73 kmh). Jackrabbits can also jump up to 20 feet (6.1 m) in a single jump. The black-tailed jackrabbit is found in the western parts of the United States and Canada, where livestock owners sometimes consider it a pest.

Description

Rabbits have some other interesting features; for instance, each eye has a field of vision of about 190 degrees, which means that rabbits can see very well in front of them, above them, and behind them. This is an especially good feature for an animal that may be preyed on by other animals, as they easily watch for any animal that may be hunting them. Rabbits' eyes are much more light-sensitive than human eyes. Their sensitivity to light is about eight times greater than ours. Although we think of animals as color-blind, there is some evidence that rabbits may be able to see blue and green.

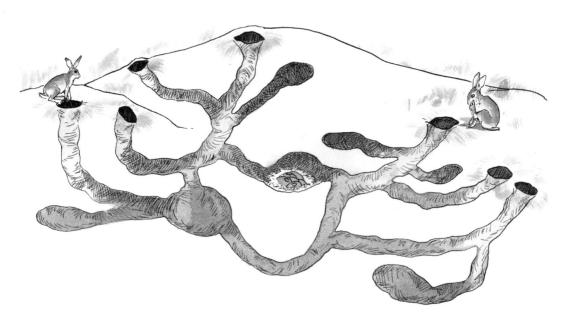

A typical rabbit warren.

Life Expectancy

Different rabbit breeds have different life expectancies, and, of course, any number is just an average. Rabbits should be expected to live at least 5 years; they can live as long as 15 years. Medium- and large-sized rabbits tend to live longer than dwarf rabbits. Breeding rabbits can easily produce litters until they are three to four years old. Some does will have litters when they are even older.

Rabbit Warrens

Wild rabbits live in groups called warrens and each warren is a system of burrows. Although warrens can be exceptionally large, each social group is usually made up of only a few males and females. A warren works together to care for the young and find food, and the rabbits in a warren also watch out for each other and warn each other when predators are near.

The females compete for the top spot in their hierarchy to get access to breeding warrens. Males compete with each other because the dominant male has breeding privileges. This competition between males often involves fighting. An established dominant male does not often have to fight to retain his position. He is also responsible for marking the group's territory, which he does by scent-marking with urine, feces, and glandular secretions.

Rabbits and Easter

Rabbits have long been associated with the Christian Easter, an annual feast commemorating the resurrection of Jesus Christ. It falls on a Sunday between March 22 and April 25.

Although Easter is a Christian tradition, it incorporates pre-Christian traditions, which is where the rabbit comes in. *Eastre* was the name of a Teutonic goddess of spring and fertility. Her festival was celebrated in the spring. Traditions associated with her festival include the Easter rabbit, a symbol of fertility, and colored Easter eggs. The eggs were originally painted in bright colors to represent the sunlight of spring. Because the Christian Easter holiday falls in the spring, these traditions of celebrating the spirit of spring have been carried on.

Note: This does not mean that you should bring home a baby rabbit at Easter simply to go along with the tradition. Bringing any new pet into the home is a serious and long-term commitment.

Rabbits and Dog Racing

Dog racing, as we know it today, originated as the sport of coursing in ancient Egypt. In coursing, dogs pursued live game by sight rather than scent, and live rabbits were used for the dogs to chase. Coursing was popular from its beginnings about 2500 B.C. through the Middle Ages. Coursing competitions were formally organized in Britain in the eighteenth century. The oldest and most famous of these competitions is the Waterloo Cup, held in Liverpool.

Opposition to the use of live rabbits as lures became strong by the early nineteenth century; as a result, the mechanical lure was developed in the United States. Within just a few years, greyhound racing replaced coursing in popularity both in the United States and Britain. Because of the history of the sport, the mechanical lure that greyhounds still chase around the track today is known as the "bun" or "bunny."

Rabbit Overpopulation

It is difficult to think of the world as having too many rabbits, but unfortunately, this is exactly the case in New Zealand and Australia. Rabbits are not native to either country. They were introduced by European settlers. In 1850 three pairs of rabbits brought by British settlers were released in Australia. Around 1860 rabbits were released on Rangitata Island, New Zealand and by 1876 a Parliamentary committee was already investigating the rabbit nuisance in New Zealand. The release of wild gray rabbits near Carterton in 1870 started the plague on the North Island of New Zealand. By the end of that century, rabbits were known throughout the country.

Because rabbits in the wild bear four to eight litters a year, with three to eight kits per litter, the number of rabbits rapidly escalated. The rabbit had no natural predators in Australia and only one—the native falcon— in New Zealand, so the growth of the rabbit population continued unabated. The rabbits naturally ate whatever vegetation was available, which, unfortunately, often meant the destruction of crops and gardens and native vegetation. As a result, farmers suffered and native wildlife populations were negatively affected.

Controlling the Rabbit Population in New Zealand

In New Zealand, hundreds of millions of dollars have been spent trying to gain the upper hand on the rabbit overpopulation. Since only the native falcon naturally preyed on rabbits, other animals that prey on rabbits, such as the cat and ferret, were imported and used to reduce the rabbit population. Between 1884 and 1886 alone, 4,000 ferrets, 3,099 weasels, and 137 stoats were released, but the predators alone did not control the rabbit population. People used guns, poisons, and traps to kill the now-wild rabbits. The rabbit population had seemed under control in New Zealand as a result of the many measures used until the 1940s, when the population exploded again. In 1947 the Rabbit Nuisance Amendment Act was passed declaring all-out war on rab-

The English Lop's huge ears usually stop growing at about 4 months of age.

bits. Although total eradication of the rabbit in New Zealand seemed possible by 1959, as the population dropped, farmers became complacent. As a result, they have not been eradicated and, since then, New Zealand has changed its policy and no longer seeks total eradication of the rabbit population.

Tuberculosis and poison bait: New Zealand ferrets are now widely infected with tuberculosis; as a result, they will not be as effective as predators in helping to control the rabbit population. There is also the concern, of course, of how the tuberculosis will affect rabbits, cattle, and farmers. New Zealand will likely have

to take steps to control the ferret population so that they do not pass tuberculosis on to the cattle.

Another problem for New Zealand is that a poison, 1080, was used to kill rabbits. Some groups of rabbits avoided the poisonous bait and many people questioned the use of poison in this country with its sparkly green image.

Today, the wild rabbit population costs New Zealanders $22 million a year in control measures and $8 million a year in lost production. Viruses that infect and kill rabbits are now being used to help manage the population. These viruses are not known to affect any other species.

Overpopulation in Australia

In Australia, rabbits destroy more than $600 million worth of food and pasture every year. They have been labeled the "chainsaws of the Outback," and millions of dollars were spent to kill the rabbits and protect the crops. In order to control this growing problem, Australian scientists released the myxoma virus in the 1950s. This virus (discussed fully on page 66) is transmitted by mosquitoes and kills rabbits without harming other animals. The release of the myxoma virus did help reduce the rabbit population, but not to the degree that the Australians needed.

In the 1990s Australian scientists released another rabbit virus for further control. This time, they released the rabbit calicivirus, which is thought to affect only rabbits and does not require an insect to transmit it. Rabbits pass this virus to other rabbits. The virus now follows a two-year cycle. It kills up to 90 percent of adult rabbits but not young rabbits. Young rabbits, up to eight weeks old, do not often die from the virus; instead, they develop antibodies and become immune. The following year, these immune rabbits bear their own young and pass on temporary immunity. Because their immunity does not last through adulthood, this generation of rabbits is susceptible to the calicivirus and is likely to die from it. Since the release of the calicivirus, the rabbit population has dropped dramatically in Australia. In some areas, the number of rabbits dropped by 90 percent and plants and animals that had not been seen in these areas for years have begun to reappear. Scientists are also studying the effects of predators on the rabbit population. They want to be sure that any changes they make will not harm the ecosystem more than it already is.

Fertility control: Australian scientists continue to monitor the rabbit population closely and are studying effective methods of fertility control in rabbits. Unfortunately, it does not appear that fertility control will be an effective way to minimize the rabbit population. When some of the females in warrens were spayed so they could not reproduce, those females lived longer and contributed to loss of vegetation for years longer. Scientists also found that more of the kits born to the females that were not spayed survived, probably because there were fewer food demands on the warren with fewer kits being born at any time. Because a greater portion of the kits survived, the overall population did not decrease as expected.

Rabbit Underpopulation

In the United States, there are areas that used to have large numbers of native wild rabbits but that now have quite small populations. In some areas, there is actually a risk of rabbits becoming endangered; for

Rabbit Tidbits

• There is no record as to why a rabbit's foot is a symbol of good luck, but it is commonly known to be a lucky token.

• Rabbits have a split upper lip. When a human is born with a split upper lip instead of a full lip, it is called a harelip.

• Rabbits keep the same coat color all year-round. Some hares are colored in the summer, but develop a white coat in the winter.

• Rabbits are only rabbits to us. Around the world, they are known by many different names:

Arabic	*ameb* or *araanib*
Czech	*kralik* or *kracilek* (little rabbit)
Chinese	*Pak Toi* (white rabbit), *Yah Toi* (wild rabbit), *Toi Bao Bao* (baby rabbit), or *Toi Tsai* (old grumpy rabbit)
Danish	*kanin*
Dutch	*konijn* or *konijntje*
Finnish	*Jsnis*
French	*le lapin* or *la lapine*
German	*des kaninchen*
Greek	*kouneli*
Hebrew	*arnevet* or *shafan*
Irish	*coinin*
Italian	*il coniglio* or *il coniglietto*
Japanese	*usagi*
Korean	*Toki*
Norwegian	*kanin*
Polish	*kro'lik* or *kroliczek*
Russian	*krolik* or *zayets*
Spanish	*conejo* or *conejito* (little rabbit)
Swedish	*kanin*

example, New England cottontail rabbits are New England's only indigenous rabbits. A New Hampshire wildlife ecologist reports that over the past 40 years, the New England cottontail has lost 80 percent of its habitat due to land development and the maturation of the forests. As a result, the cottontail population is fading fast. Unfortunately, this cottontail, as opposed to some other cottontail breeds, has not been very good at adapting to new areas or environments. In 1960 the New England cottontail was known through all of the New England states, but in the 1990s it has apparently vanished from Vermont altogether, and has become scarce in Maine and New Hampshire.

Although other rabbits may appear, the New England cottontail may now be one of New England's most endangered mammals.

Rabbit Uses

Animal Experimentation

As early as the second century, we know that animals were used as subjects in medical experiments. In this century, and even today, scientists use laboratory animals to study biological processes in animals and humans, and to study the causes of disease. Animals have been used to test surgical techniques and drugs and to evaluate the safety of chemicals used in products that humans will come in contact with.

Rabbits make up a very small percentage of the animals that are used in experimentation, and even that number is falling. The Mississippi State Extension Service estimates that 600,000 rabbits a year are currently used. Scientists are developing other ways to gather needed information without animal experimentation. Rabbits were perhaps most commonly used to test chemicals that may be irritating to the skin of humans. For example, since rabbits have a similar sensitivity to that of humans, cosmetics were placed in or around a rabbit's eyes (the Draize eye irritancy test), or on the rabbit's skin, and the rabbit was monitored for any irritation or reaction. If the rabbit had a reaction to a chemical, it would be likely that a human would also have a reaction. Irritating chemicals do not make it to market. Today, cell and tissue cultures can be used to test for irritation and reactivity instead, which means that many fewer rabbits are being used for research and cosmetic testing. When you see a skin or cosmetics product labeled "No animal testing was done," you can rest assured that no rabbits were harmed to test that product.

Wool Production

The primary wool breed of rabbit is the Angora. Its wool can be sheared or plucked three to four times a year. One rabbit will produce anywhere from $\frac{1}{2}$ to $1\frac{1}{2}$ pounds (0.1–0.7 kg) of wool a year. Although this does not seem like a lot of fur based on the weight, keep in mind that hair is very lightweight, so this is actually a considerable amount of wool. Angora wool can be knitted into warm blankets and garments.

Meat and Fur Production

Meat rabbits are primarily raised for human consumption, although there are some specialty rabbit-based foods made for cats and dogs. Rabbits raised for their meat tend to be medium- to large-sized rabbits with a high proportion of muscle for their size. In the United States, the last available estimate of how much rabbit meat is consumed each year is from 1977. The estimate was that 10 to 12 million pounds, some imported, are eaten each year in the United States.

Although rabbits that are classified as meat breeds are primarily used for meat production, the meat from any rabbit is edible. Rabbit meat is easy to digest and rich in protein. Due to breeding, lifestyle, and diet, the meat from a domestic rabbit will be more tender and have a higher fat content than the meat of a wild rabbit.

Some rabbits have been raised for their pelts, which are usually used to make fur coats. The Rex and Satin breeds have pelts that are especially desirable to furriers. Their pelts are not usually treated before they are made into garments, while the fur of other breeds is often processed to form a finished product. Typically, white rabbits are raised, so the fur can be stippled or dyed to match any known fur. Breeding rabbits specifically for their pelts is not a large business in the United States.

According to the Mississippi State Extension Service, 6 to 8 million rabbits are raised in the United States each year for production purposes, down from a peak production of 24 million rabbits in 1944.

Jackalope— Fact or Fiction?

It is hard to tell how this particular myth got started, but, however it began, it has amused patrons in restaurants, bars, and shops

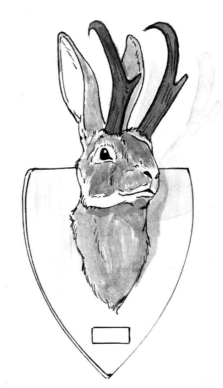

The mythical (or is it?) jackalope.

throughout the country. Patrons may notice the mounted head of the jackalope on a wall with its jackrabbit head and antelopelike horns, the result of laborious crossbreeding by the taxidermist. The jackalope is a legend that goes back centuries and exists in countries other than the United States. It most likely started because tumors or growths that occurred on the heads of jackrabbits made them appear to be growing horns. The papillomavirus is known to cause growths in the neck and ear regions. No horns actually grow.

Chapter Two

Selecting a Pet Rabbit

Do Rabbits Make Good Pets?

Rabbits make wonderful pets. Each rabbit has a distinct personality, just as different people or dogs or cats do. You can enjoy teaching them and playing games with them. Yes, rabbits *can* be trained. They can learn commands, games, and even to use a litter box. They can also teach you a game or two.

Here are some facts about rabbits:
• Rabbits in the United States do not need vaccinations, so they do not require frequent visits to the veterinarian.
• Rabbits make little noise. You will not need to worry about your neighbor calling to complain in the middle of the night because of barking or yowling. That is not to say that your rabbit will not talk to you, because he will—especially when he is annoyed with you.
• Compared to other caged pets, rabbits tend to be tamer and more trainable. When the children want to cuddle with a rabbit, the rabbit is more likely to tolerate, and even enjoy, it.

• Rabbits enjoy socializing and playing games. Too often, other caged pets do not enjoy being handled and petted and would rather be left alone.
• Compared to dogs or cats, rabbits are not very demanding, and cost less to keep. Your rabbit will not grab a leash and pester you mercilessly during your favorite TV show for a walk outside.
• As a rule, rabbits cost less to feed and care for; you will not have to commit part of your budget to vaccines and heartworm preventive.
• Since there are so many varieties and sizes of rabbits to choose from, it would be almost impossible not to find one that would fit into your family. Small or big, longhaired or short, floppy ears or straight . . . you have a lot of choices.

Is a Rabbit Right for You?

So, you think you would like to have a rabbit? Perhaps you are planning to add a new one to the household. There is no single type of rabbit that is right for everyone. There is a wide range of breeds to choose from in different sizes, shapes, temperaments, and colors (see Rabbit Breeds, page 100). You can get an eight-week-old Mini Lop or a four-year-old sleek Lilac Himalayan. You also need to choose a male or a female, and decide whether you should get one or more.

As pets, rabbits are great companions that want to have fun with you and even learn from you. However, there are aspects of a rabbit's personality that are not so appealing. For instance, rabbits love to chew and have to be monitored and trained so that they do not chew on carpets, baseboards, and electrical wires. Some rabbits do not like to be cuddled; others are easily frightened, and may bite or run as a result. When you are choosing a rabbit, try to pick one that has been handled and does not seem overly anxious.

Rabbits are not very demanding, so they tend to make good pets.

Is Your Family Ready for a Rabbit?

Before adding any pet to your household, be sure that you and your family are ready for the financial and time responsibilities. Rabbits should never be obtained on impulse. Unfortunately, people who do bring rabbits home on impulse often are not able to get their rabbits off to a good start and if rabbits are not fed properly and protected from injury, they become ill, even critically so, quickly. The last thing you want is to end up at the veterinary hospi-

tal with a sick rabbit the day after bringing him home.

It is time to ask yourself some honest questions: Will my other pets learn to accept a new rabbit? Who will be responsible for the cage cleaning every day? Can I be sure the rabbit will be fed twice a day? Can I afford a pet, including the cost of veterinary care?

Children

Consider a rabbit as a pet very carefully if you have very young children; as a general rule, rabbits are not good pets for children under the age of seven. Rabbits, especially the smaller breeds, are physically delicate and can be easily injured by children. If your children are at the age where they are likely to suddenly grab for or pick up the rabbit, they may frighten the rabbit and cause him to kick and struggle. This would cause very serious injuries to a rabbit, not to mention the fact that your child may be scratched or bitten.

If your children are old enough to handle a rabbit responsibly, you must still be sure that the rabbit's care is not entirely left to the children. Rabbits are very prone to stress and illness with changes in their routines or feedings. They must be monitored for subtle signs of illness. For these reasons, it is best to double-check your child's feeding and maintenance of the rabbit every day and to observe the rabbit yourself for any change that may indicate a health problem. I have had many mothers in my exam room share their frustration by saying, "Of course my eight-year-old daughter promised to take full responsibility for this pet, but after a few weeks, I could tell she wasn't keeping her part of the bargain."

Larger breeds of rabbits are generally better for children. Many people are tempted to get the dwarf or smaller breeds for young children because they are cute and easy to carry. However, they are at greater risk of injury from children just because of their smaller size. Leg and back fractures, particularly, occur when a rabbit is mishandled. Medium- and large-breed rabbits tend to be less excitable and aggressive than the dwarf breeds.

Even with these guidelines, you must ultimately decide if your child is ready. Some eight-year-olds would provide more diligent care than some teenagers. Some toddlers have already been taught to be very gentle with the family cat and not pick him up. That toddler would be at lower risk for injuring a rabbit or being hurt by a rabbit.

Finding the Right Rabbit

When you are sure a rabbit is right for your family and you have worked out who will care for the rabbit, it is time to go get one. There are several places to look:

1. If you are looking for a young rabbit or specific breed of rabbit, your best bet is to visit local breeders or pet stores. To help find the best source in your area, contact the local rabbit club and ask for a list of reputable breeders and pet stores in your area. Rabbit clubs may be listed in the phone book, on the Internet, or with the American Rabbit Breeders Association (ARBA) (see Information, page 131).

2. Another good way to learn about different breeds and meet breeders is to go to local 4H and agricultural fairs. These fairs will have a house or barn where they have show rabbits on display and breeders or rabbit club members available to answer your questions.

3. Some shelters and rescue groups will occasionally have a rabbit among the dogs and cats you expect them to have. Recently, my local shelter had a rabbit dropped

If you're considering buying a rabbit for a young child, it's important to teach the child proper care procedures.

off—24 hours later, she gave birth to four more. The shelter staff had to learn about raising rabbits fast! I am happy to report that the shelter arranged for homes for all of them.

4. Owners no longer able to keep their rabbits may place advertisements in the local paper looking for a new home.

What Breed?

It can be exceedingly difficult to narrow your choices down to one breed; however, if you attend a rabbit show, you will not only be able to see what breeds appeal to you, you will also be able to talk to breeders about the care of the rabbit. If this is your first rabbit, I would not recommend a high-maintenance breed such as the Angora. The Netherland Dwarf and the lop-eared rabbits are very popular in the United States and do not have high maintenance requirements.

Pedigrees

If you obtain a pedigreed rabbit from a reputable rabbit breeder, you will have some assurances about your pet. You will know that the breeder produces rabbits that meet the Standard of Perfection for their breed and get some indication as to the health of the rabbit. A grade rabbit is a rabbit without a pedigree. Grade rabbits are often the result of crossbreeding between different breeds—mixed-breed rabbits. They will not have been selectively bred for the best traits of a breed. A grade rabbit should not be chosen if you have any interest in showing your rabbit.

Registered Adults

If you want even more assurances about the rabbit that you select, you can purchase a registered adult. An ARBA-licensed registrar has examined a registered rabbit and has determined that the rabbit is in good health and is a good representative of his breed. If a rabbit does not meet these qualifications, he will not be registered. You should expect to pay more for a registered rabbit or one that is carefully bred. You can get more information on pedigrees, registering, and the ARBA by reading the chapter on showing rabbits (see page 94).

Visiting the Rabbitry

Do not commit to purchasing a rabbit before you have a chance to see him and the environment in which he is kept. One way to get more information before you select a rabbit is to call a breeder and say that you are thinking about getting a rabbit and would like some information. Ask if you can come and see the breeder's rabbitry, the place where rabbits are kept or raised. Take a good look at both the rabbit and his environment. If you are able to visit an entire litter of rabbits, look to see that all the kits appear healthy. There should not be any runts—any kits that are obviously less developed than the others. Young rabbits should be active and plump but not potbellied. Their coats should have a fine sheen and not be matted in any way. A rabbit's body should appear "balanced."

All the rabbits should be in a clean environment with fresh water and food available. If the rabbit is not kept in clean and proper conditions, your chance of getting a rabbit with problems increases. If the breeder has a lot of rabbits, they should all be housed in separate cages with enough room in each cage so that each rabbit does not seem cramped. Ask the caretaker whether any rabbits in the line, or any rabbits in contact with the rabbit you want, have had Pasteurella or coccidia. Good breeding and environmental management can possibly eliminate coccidia, but it is estimated that as high as 85 percent of the rabbit population carries Pasteurella multocida. Never feel pressured to buy or take a rabbit just because you are there.

Evaluating a Rabbit

Now look at the rabbit you are thinking of bringing into your home and family.
• Is he active and bright-eyed?
• Is his coat in good condition?
• Are his eyes and nose free of any discharge?
• Does the rabbit have a normal bite as opposed to a malocclusion (see page 63)?
• Does the body appear balanced and in good condition?
• Is the bottom of the rabbit's foot well padded with fur, not bare or raw?
• Are the insides of the ears clean?
• Does the rabbit look like what a member of his breed should look like?
• Does the rabbit appear to be eating well and not potbellied or thin?

• If the answer to all these questions is yes, then it sounds like you are off to a good start.

What to Consider Before Buying a Rabbit

Young or Adult?

Consider whether you want a young rabbit or an adult. Kits should not be taken away from their mother and siblings until they are about eight weeks old and on solid food. With a young rabbit, you will get to enjoy watching him grow up, but a young rabbit will also be more active. The downside of young rabbits is that they require more monitoring because young rabbits chew and chew and chew, and you need to change their diet as they age. A chewing rabbit can be frustrating. Novice rabbit owners have had baseboards ruined and computer or phone wires chewed up before they caught on.

Adult rabbits tend to be less active and easier to train, especially if they are neutered. Depending on where you get an adult rabbit from, he may come with housing or equipment and with some training. Adult rabbits may already have been spayed or neutered, which would avoid that expense for you.

One or More?

In the wild, rabbits live in groups called warrens (see page 3). They interact to raise their young and to find food. They keep watch for each other and warn the rest of the warren when predators are approaching. Single rabbits, therefore, can feel isolated and get into more trouble. Pairs of rabbits will often form strong bonds with each other and relate better to people, especially a male and female or two females. One study showed that when two females were able to choose whether to be alone or together, they chose to spend 90 percent of their time together. This does not apply to a pair of males, who will likely be very aggressive toward each other and injure each other, especially if they are not neutered.

Dogs: Although many dogs are capable of getting along with a rabbit, many are not. Many breeds including terriers, hounds, and sporting dogs are natural hunters. A Westie or Scottie, for example, would think rabbit chasing is good sport. You do not want your rabbit to live in constant terror, or worse, be killed by your dog. A distraught client called me one day because he had adopted a Greyhound the day before, and while he was away at work, the Greyhound had attacked the rabbit cage attempting to get to the rabbits. One of his rabbits died trying to escape from the dog.

Male or Female?

If you decide to get two rabbits, a male and female will have the closest bond. You may put two females together, but never put two males

Keeping two rabbits as pets often allows them to form strong bonds with one another.

together. Although large groups of males and females live together in a warren, the males often fight with one another to improve their position in the hierarchy. Males will do the same in your home. They will fight with each other and cause serious injuries that can be fatal. Males that have been neutered may be able to get along, but even if two males seem to get along well, you cannot trust them to never fight with each other.

One evening, a client brought a male rabbit into the emergency hospital where I was working. She kept two male rabbits at the ice cream stand she owned. Each had his own hutch. That night, a customer had opened the hutches and put the two rabbits in together. Sadly, she did not know it until she heard them fighting. The rabbit she brought in for treatment had actually been castrated by the other rabbit. It was a hard lesson learned and one you should take to heart; two males that have not been neutered may fight very hard.

As a rule, one sex does not make a better pet than the other unless you are considering how one sex will fit into a household with other pets or other rabbits. Whether you get a male or female, it is best to have him or her neutered or spayed by an experienced veterinarian. The rabbit will be healthier and have less stress. Neutering males will also keep them from marking their territory with urine.

Bringing a Rabbit Home

Now that you have found the perfect companion, let's see how you can make the transition smooth for everyone. It is best to have all the equipment you need before you bring the rabbit home. The cage or hutch should be set up in advance. You should have some good-quality rabbit pellets and fresh hay ready, as well as water sippers and food bowls. Ideally, you will even be prepared with a litter box, if you want your rabbit to use one, and toys.

The Veterinarian

There are some other things that will help you be prepared for every contingency. If you do not already have a relationship with a veterinarian who takes care of rabbits, at least try to get the phone number of one before you bring your rabbit home. The first time you live with another species you are not familiar with can be very stressful. Most of the stress comes from not knowing what is normal and what is abnormal. For instance, you worry about whether you are feeding correctly and whether the room temperature is right; you hear your rabbit make some sounds for the first time and you do not know if he is talking to you or if he is in pain. You need to have a medical expert available if you think there may be a problem. The breeder will also be a good resource if you have a general question rather than one about a potential medical problem.

Food

Find out from the breeder or pet store salesperson or prior caregiver what your rabbit has been eating. Rabbits can get very ill from fast changes in their diet. It is always best for the first few days to keep feeding the rabbit what he has already been eating. It is okay to offer him unlimited amounts of hay. Once your rabbit is adjusted to your home, you can begin to make any feeding changes that are necessary. Read the Nutrition chapter (page 41) to learn what is best for your rabbit at his age. Make any changes very slowly. Take days or even weeks to make adjustments so that your rabbit will not get sick from a quick change.

Adjusting Slowly

It is easy to overwhelm your new rabbit when you bring him home; everybody wants to shower him with attention and affection. You want to teach him everything he needs to know right away, but go slowly. This precious little rabbit has a big adjustment to make. He is being taken away from the life he knows and is being put in a new one. He will need some time to adjust. Let your rabbit spend time in his cage, and at certain times leave the door open so your rabbit can choose to come out and interact with you. If you force your rabbit to interact with you before he is comfortable, you may get a reaction you do not want—he may run or thump or kick. You want your new pet to trust you and he will not trust

It's important to exercise caution when introducing a new rabbit to an existing pet in your home.

take days or months depending on the personalities of your pets. Continue to allow your rabbit and other pets to see each other without having any direct contact. You can even feed your pets special treats when they behave well together. Do not underestimate the power of rewards and bribery. In the beginning, behaving nicely may simply mean that they do not act hostile to each other.

When your pets seem comfortable in each other's presence, it is time to expand the introduction. Have both pets restrained in some fashion and let them sniff each other. If that goes well, put them on the floor together. Supervise them closely. You should get involved as soon as there is any sign of danger to one of your pets by separating them. Gradually increase the amount of time you let them spend together. Once they get along, you can just sit back and enjoy watching their interactions and shenanigans.

Introducing Rabbits to Each Other

"I'm so glad I brought another rabbit home. My other rabbit took to her right away and now they're almost inseparable."

"I'll tell you, I almost wish I hadn't gotten another rabbit now. My first rabbit, Buster, is so angry he doesn't want anything to do with the new guy. He keeps chasing him away."

Either of these scenarios is possible when you first put rabbits together. A proper introduction is important.

you if you scare or overwhelm him. He may even run from you or become aggressive. Of course, you may bring home such a social rabbit that he wants to spend all his time with you right from the beginning.

Other Pets

Do not assume that your rabbit will make instant friends with the other pets in your house. Make sure that any other pets are not allowed in your rabbit's cage so that your rabbit will feel secure in his cage and not worry that it will be invaded. Allow other pets to come up to the side of your rabbit's cage while he is inside. If there are any signs of hostility, do not let the introduction go any further until it stops, which could

You will not need to spend much time introducing rabbits to each other when both are new; there are few that will not adjust quickly. Introducing a new rabbit to one or more that are already in the house and have established a territory can be more complicated.

The easiest introductions will be between females and males. Even when a doe and buck do not immediately take to each other, there is rarely any significant trouble between them, but introducing members of the same sex can be an entirely different story. Females may get along from the start, or they may fight, while fighting is very common among males introduced to each other. I do not recommend allowing two intact (not neutered) males to have any contact with each other, but two neutered males may be able to get along.

Keep in mind that rabbits are very territorial. A first introduction should take place in a neutral space that no rabbit considers his territory. A room your rabbit has not been in or a new pen in the yard may be good options. You can also introduce them outside your home altogether to prevent any territorial feelings.

Any interactions at first should be well supervised. Do not interfere with the meeting unless there are true signs of aggression. Give them a chance to work things out on their own. If one rabbit wants nothing to do with the other, or if they fight, you will need to make a more gradual introduction. Try to break up a fight with a spray of water before jumping in yourself.

If your first rabbit is anxious about the new addition, you can help relieve the anxiety by making sure that positive things happen when the new rabbit is around. For example, if your rabbit especially enjoys being rubbed in a certain area, rub him while you let the other rabbit move around the room. You can also give the rabbits treats when they are near each other. The idea is for the rabbits to associate positive experiences with being together.

For rabbits that want to fight with each other, you will need to set aside time every day to supervise them in neutral territory. You might start by having the rabbits on opposite sides of a gate, so they can see each other but not interact. Make sure you reward them for good behavior and correct bad behavior. Bad behavior, such as lunging for the other rabbit, can be corrected with a loud voice or noise or a spray of water. As the rabbits learn to accept each other, or at least ignore each other, you can give them more time together with no barriers between them. Do not leave them together unsupervised until you are absolutely sure they will no longer fight.

Chapter Three

Caring for Your Rabbit

Your beautiful new rabbit has been welcomed into your home—an exciting new arrival. You can't wait to share your news with family and friends. But, now what do you do with him? Do you keep him in his cage? Do you let him run free? I can just see your new little friend inspecting your expensive stereo equipment with his teeth.

Handling

Contrary to rumor, rabbits should never be picked up by their ears alone. Whenever a rabbit is picked up, it is important to fully support him so that he will feel secure. If the rabbit is frightened or unstable when he is picked up, he may bite, scratch, or try to escape. A rabbit that kicks hard with his rear legs while being held or picked up risks fracturing his back. A rabbit's skeleton is very delicate and brittle. This increases his chance for injury. Also, some rabbits will become relaxed if cradled on their backs with the head tipped gently backward. This is often

A member of the Rex breed.

the easiest way to trim nails or clean sensitive areas.

How to Pick Up Your Rabbit

A rabbit that is not used to being picked up may run away or attack you when you try to pick him up. There are two methods of properly picking up a rabbit:

1. Start by petting him. Use one hand to grab the rabbit by the scruff and the other hand to support his back legs. The hand supporting the back legs should be supporting the weight of the rabbit and you should be holding the head higher than the body. Move the first hand from the scruff to under the chest. The rabbit is then carried in front of you.

2. The other method is to pick the rabbit up and cradle him against your body. Use your arms to provide support underneath the rabbit and on the side away from your body so that the rabbit cannot jump.

Note: If a rabbit is especially anxious or likely to squirm and jump, you may want to wrap him in a towel or small blanket before picking him up. Do not wrap up your rabbit for an extended period of time or he will develop heat stress.

The proper way to pick up and hold your rabbit.

Rabbit-proofing Your Home

If you thought child-proofing a home was difficult, consider the problem of rabbit-proofing. It takes some practice to start thinking at floor level about potential dangers. Rabbit-proofing your home involves eliminating danger for the rabbit as well as protecting your property from damage.

Electrical Cords

The most important things to watch out for are electrical cords. Rabbits will chew on them and get an electric shock. If your rabbit gets a severe enough shock, he may burn his tongue, or even die; therefore, precautions should be taken before a rabbit is ever let loose in a room in your home. Cords can be hidden by running them under carpeting or behind furniture, or wrapped inside plastic tubing. At hardware stores, you can buy pre-slit tubing into which you can slide the cord. You can also buy tubing at a hardware or aquarium store that you can slit lengthwise yourself. Simply tuck the wire into the slit to cover the wire with protective tubing. There is another product called spiral cable wrap that can also be used to wrap electrical and phone cords.

Houseplants

Many houseplants have toxic properties when eaten by your rabbit (see page 130). Although some of them cause mild symptoms, it is best to keep your rabbit from chewing on any houseplant. If your rabbit seems interested in your plants, hang them high or put them in an area your rabbit cannot access.

Wood Furniture and Baseboards

Protecting your wood furniture and baseboards from a chewing rabbit requires training. You will also need to be sure to provide items that your rabbit is allowed to chew. Anytime your rabbit starts chewing inappropriately, tell him firmly to stop and offer him an acceptable toy or block of wood. Never underestimate the chewing potential of a young, active rabbit.

You may also want to keep your rabbit from going under the furniture so that he cannot chew up the upholstery and filling and cannot urinate or defecate under the furniture. You can use cardboard or wood to make a frame under the furniture that is not visible to people but will prevent the rabbit from getting too far underneath.

Home Temperatures

Inside the home, it is best to keep your rabbit in areas that are between 60 and 70°F (16–21°C). Rabbits can tolerate temperatures as low as 40°F (4.4°C) if they are not suddenly moved from a warm environment to a cold one.

Rabbit Cages

This section talks about cages for transporting or for rabbits inside the home. Cages for outdoor rabbits are hutches and are described separately (see page 26).

Cages for Transporting

A cage for transporting a rabbit should not be very large because you do not want your rabbit sliding around inside it. A car ride can be scary enough without having the rabbit thrown off balance. A kennel cab that is used for a dog or cat can be used for a rabbit too. You can also get a small wire or wood cage. Your rabbit may handle a trip in his cage better if you put in some hay and pellets or vegetables and a water bottle, but do not be surprised if he is reluctant to eat or drink in a transport cage. Also, place an absorbent towel in the bottom of the cage to catch any urine or feces; this will keep your rabbit cleaner and make your cleanup job easier.

Cages for Inside the Home

A cage for your rabbit inside the home should be much larger than the transport cage. Your rabbit will be spending a lot of time here. It should be large enough for a litter box area, a feeding area, and room to sleep and move around. The cage should be at least four times the size of your rabbit. If you choose a cage with a wire bottom, you will not need a litter box area; instead, you will have a pan underneath the entire cage that will collect urine, feces, falling hay, bedding, and food. The wire must have a relatively fine mesh and be smooth in order to prevent injury to your rabbit's feet. You

The cage should be at least four times the size of your rabbit.

should provide a solid area of flooring with a board over the wire floor for your rabbit's comfort. During his training, your rabbit should be kept in the cage whenever you cannot closely supervise him.

Building your own: You may choose to build your own rabbit cage, or you can modify a commercial cage. Building plans for rabbit cages can be obtained from state extension services or agricultural offices. Do not use a glass cage or aquarium because there will not be enough ventilation. Rabbits enjoy ramps or steps and a platform area. When rabbits are offered two levels to live on, they usually spend an equal amount of time on the top and bottom levels.

Feeders and waterers: Placing your rabbit's food in a feeder rather than on the cage floor will keep the food and the cage cleaner. It will also help you track how well your rabbit is eating.

Wooden feeders are not a good choice since rabbits often chew on the wood. Metal feeders, ceramic crocks, or nontipping plastic crocks are all good choices. You can purchase a metal self-feeder made to hang on the side of a rabbit's cage. These feeders can be accessed from outside the cage and require the least cleaning and maintenance.

Water can also be left in a crock or plastic bowl that cannot be tipped over. Polyvinyl crocks are preferable because they are easier to clean, do not rust, do not readily harbor bacteria, and will not break if frozen in the winter. Many people find sipper bottles that are attached to the side of the cage easier to use. Both bottles and bowls need to be rinsed and refilled at least once a day. You must make sure that your rabbit always has fresh water available. For outdoor rabbits in the summer, you may have to fill the water container more than once a day. In the winter, you will need to check that the water has not become frozen. At least once a week, the water container should be cleaned with a very dilute bleach solution and then rinsed thoroughly.

Bedding: Stock the cage with comfortable bedding. Also, a piece of wood attached to the cage is helpful for chewing. For bedding, you can use straw, hay, a sheepskin rug, or even a towel. Just make sure that your rabbit does not eat any fabric or rug that you put in the cage.

Note: Your rabbit should be made to feel that this cage area is his own private sanctuary; therefore, never punish your rabbit by putting him in his cage and never trap him in his cage.

Cleaning the Cage

Clean the cage and food dishes while the rabbit is not in his cage. Food dishes can also be attached to the door so you do not have to invade the cage to get to them. Ideally, you will be able to allow your rabbit to go in and out of the cage on his own. If the cage has a raised door that your rabbit cannot reach on his own, provide a stable ramp or step for him to use to get in and out. When you need to put your rabbit back in the cage, you can herd him toward the door.

Herding: To herd a rabbit, stand behind him and clap your hands or "shoo" him toward the cage. Some rabbits have been able to learn verbal commands. You may be able to teach yours a command to come out and one to go in.

Toys

Toys? For a rabbit? Absolutely. The proper toys will help keep your rabbit active and occupied, and keep him out of trouble. He will be less likely to get bored and need to explore and destroy your home. Your rabbit will help guide you to the type of toy that is best for his age. Be careful not to leave plastic toys around that your rabbit can eat.

Some toys that your rabbit can chew on are appropriate, such as untreated wood that has been aged a few months or cardboard rolls from inside paper towels or toilet paper. Simple things such as cardboard boxes and paper bags can be entertaining for a rabbit to crawl in, scratch on, and chew. You can build your own tunnels, mazes, or play gyms for your rabbit. PVC pipes are often used. Be careful to choose the correct size so your rabbit cannot get stuck inside. Some rabbit owners have become very creative designing and building their own rabbit play gyms complete with a variety of surfaces, levels, and attached toys or chew items. Some rabbit toys are as simple as a box within a box, both boxes with multiple openings. Your rabbit may enjoy tossing an empty soda can around—just make sure there are no sharp edges.

Toys made for cats and birds can be appropriate. Choose toys that can be hit or tossed. Do not choose anything your rabbit may eat a piece out of that might cause gastrointestinal problems. Untreated wicker and paper can also be very entertaining for a rabbit, as can an empty coconut shell. When choosing toys, be creative but consider your rabbit's safety.

Rabbit Hutches

A hutch is a rabbit's outdoor home. Carefully reconsider getting a rabbit at all if you plan to keep it out-

"Toys" for your rabbit can be as simple as branches or paper bags.

doors all the time. Outdoor rabbits will not be as good pets as indoor rabbits; they will also be exposed to predators even if kept in a safe hutch and can die from stress under a hutch attack by a predator such as a raccoon or a dog. They can severely injure themselves trying to stay away from the predator. Having said all that, rabbits *can* live outdoors even in the winter. They must be protected from temperatures below 40°F (4.4°C) and above 85°F (29.4°C).

You must build a hutch properly to protect your rabbit. It should be several feet off the ground and on a stable base. It should face the morning sun, not the afternoon sun, if possible. It can contain one or two areas; two areas are a must if you have a female that is bred.

Nesting area: One area should be enclosed except for a small entry door. This enclosed area is where you should put bedding (straw or hay) for the rabbit to nest in.

Feeding and relief areas: The other area is used for feeding and "bathroom duties," and should be made with galvanized fine-mesh wire.

Flooring: There should be some give to the flooring. A ½- to 1-inch (1.3–2.5-cm) 14-gauge wire floor works well. The holes should be large enough to drop feces through, but not large enough for your rabbit to hurt his feet or for a predator to get a mouth or paw in. Or, you can make the entire bottom of the hutch a solid floor, which will minimize drafts and reduce the risk of sore feet, but will require more care to keep clean.

Size and Materials

The hutch should be large enough to allow the rabbit to move around. A standard rule is to provide a square foot (78 cm^2) of clear floor space for every pound of adult rabbit weight. This size has been determined based on recommended sizes for breeding pens. Based on that rule, the average-sized hutch for a standard 10-pound (4.5-kg) rabbit would be 7.5 square feet, 30 inches by 36 inches (2.29 m^2, 76 cm × 91 cm) for example. The hutch should be at least 20 inches (51 cm) high; higher is better for larger breeds of rabbits.

Many hutches are built with 16-gauge wire for the sides and tops and 14-gauge wire for the floor. Wood, except for the frame, is not a good choice as the rabbit can chew on it. Wooden legs of a hutch should be treated to prevent rotting and termites. Any wood used in the hutch itself should not be treated. Partitions between hutches or within the hutch should be of plastic or metal. The roof of the hutch should extend 7 inches (18 cm) past the edge of the hutch. It should be weatherproof and sloped to carry away any rain or snow. Provide drainage under the hutch; if water remains stagnant under the hutch, insect and sanitation problems are likely to develop.

Fenced Pens

You may also consider building a fenced pen around the cage. This

A well-constructed outdoor hutch.

will act as a small deterrent to predators and give you an area in which to exercise your rabbit, but be sure that he cannot escape from the pen and that the grass in the pen has not been treated with any pesticides.

Caring for Outdoor Rabbits

Outdoor rabbits still need daily care—fresh food and water every day and a check for signs of illness.

Winter Care

Outdoor rabbits will need to be fed more in the winter because of the extra calories they burn keeping warm. Rabbits should never be moved outdoors for the first time in the winter; being able to live in winter conditions requires an adjustment. Put extra bedding in the hutch in the winter. You might also consider moving the hutch into the garage or onto an enclosed porch for the winter. Of course, winter here presumes cold temperatures. These measures are not an issue if winter weather where you live has temperatures about 50°F (10°C).

Summer Care

Summer can be as stressful as winter for outdoor rabbits, as they do not handle heat very well. When the temperature rises to 85°F (29.4°C) or higher, your rabbit can have problems. If he gets overheated, he will need immediate medical care or he may die. Make sure there is shade over the hutch and consider putting ice packs in the hutch with the rabbit when the temperature is high (see Heatstroke, page 60).

Ventilation in a Rabbit House

Air movement through your rabbit's house is critical to get rid of gases, moisture, dust, and heat. Rabbits give off a significant amount of heat and moisture that must be removed from the house. There is also ammonia in rabbit urine that will irritate your rabbit's eyes and airways if it is not removed, predisposing him to an outbreak of respiratory illness such as Pasteurellosis.

Ventilation can be provided by using screening on the sides of the house, grills on two sides, adjustable side flaps or windows. Eight to ten complete air changes an hour within the hutch are ideal. To determine whether or not your rabbit house has sufficient ventilation, you can measure the temperature and humidity inside the house and outside the house. The humidity inside the rabbit house should not be more than 5 percent higher than the humidity of the outside air. The temperature inside the rabbit house should not be more than five degrees higher than the outside. Unless the weather is cold, you will probably want the temperature and humidity inside your rabbit's house to be lower than outside the house.

In considering ventilation and air flow through the house, be careful not to create any drafts. If air is moving at too high a speed through the rabbit house, it will create a draft that may cause your rabbit to become ill.

Warm Weather

The nostrils flare, the rabbit is breathing rapidly, and he starts to seem distressed. These are the signs of heat stress. Rabbits are very susceptible to heat stress and can die of heatstroke. Be especially cautious when the temperature rises above 85°F (29.4°C). If the weather is hot, make sure your rabbit is out of the sun and in the shade. If you do not have effective air conditioning in your house, use fans to keep your rabbit cool.

To keep your rabbit cool on a hot day, you can have him rest on tile or marble, which stays cool longer. Add ice cubes to his water or provide an ice pack for him to lie near. In hot weather, brush him every day to remove any excess hair. Mist his ears to help him dissipate heat.

If your rabbit becomes overheated, his body temperature will rise above 102°F (38.9°C). For temperatures below 104°F (40°C), you should begin to treat your rabbit for heat stress at home by placing alcohol on his feet and ears and cool (not cold) water over his body. If your rabbit's body temperature is 104°F or higher, seek emergency medical care. Rabbits can die quickly of heatstroke. For more on heatstroke, see page 60.

Litter Box Training

Not everyone chooses to litter box-train their rabbit, but it can be done. Young rabbits that are less than three months old are the easiest to train. If your rabbit has a cage in the house, the litter box can be kept in the cage. If the cage has a wire floor, you do not need a litter box; the pan underneath the wire bottom is the litter pan. Rabbits with cages should be trained to urinate and defecate in their cages. Outdoor rabbits do not need litter boxes, as they have a designated area of their hutch for this purpose.

Rabbits kept in cages will often defecate in areas of their cages outside the litter box. This should be permitted so that your rabbit will feel that this is truly *his* home and territory. Rabbits mark their territory with urine, feces, and scent from the glands under the chin.

Rabbits prefer to urinate and defecate in just a few places, usually corners. To litter box-train your rabbit outside a cage, place a shallow litter box in a corner. If your rabbit has already voided or defecated in a corner, choose that one. If the place your rabbit wants to use is not where you ultimately want the litter box to be, start it there anyway—once the rabbit has been trained to use it, you will be able to move it.

When your rabbit voids outside the litter box, clean up the urine with a paper towel and put it in the litter box. Pick up any fecal pellets and put them in the litter box as well. You want the rabbit to recognize the smells in the box to know to relieve himself there. Make sure your rabbit has access to his litter box at all times, or have more than one box available in different areas. If you catch your rabbit relieving himself outside his litter box, it is okay to give a verbal correction by quickly and forcefully saying "No" and then herding your rabbit to his litter box.

He should not be unsupervised until he is litter box-trained so that you can give constant reinforcement of this correction.

The Litter

Choose litter for the box carefully. You want something absorbent that will hide odor, but not something that may be harmful to your rabbit, as rabbits will eat some of their litter; therefore, clumping litters should not be used. You should also *not* use pine or cedar shavings or chips, litters with deodorant crystals, or corncob litter. Good choices for litter include citrus-based litters, organic litters, or litter made from paper pulp or recycled paper. Newspaper and hay can be used but need to be changed the most frequently, every day. Be sure to clean the litter box regularly for cleanliness and to prevent ammonia buildup that can be harmful to your rabbit. Depending on the type of litter you use, that may mean changes every day or every week. Feces must be removed every day.

Keep in mind that very young rabbits can take quite some time to train. Do not get discouraged—rabbits really can be trained to use a litter box. Your job will also be much easier if your rabbit is spayed or neutered. Mature rabbits that have not been spayed or neutered will mark their territory by depositing urine every place to which they have access.

Food dishes: It is hard for us to understand, but some young rabbits will urinate or defecate in their food dishes. If this happens, dump the contents of the food dish into the litter box and thoroughly clean the food dish before refilling it. Your rabbit will catch on.

Accidents

If your rabbit is litter box-trained and begins to have accidents outside the box, it can be a symptom of illness. If there is not an obvious reason for your rabbit to have stopped using the litter box, such as a frightening thing happening there, a new rabbit in the house, or an unclean box, take him to the veterinarian for a checkup.

Grooming

Rabbit breeds have four different types of hair:

1. Normal fur is a dense undercoat with coarse guard hairs extending past the undercoat.

2. Satin fur is fine and has a hair shaft that reflects light, giving it a spectacular sheen.

3. Rex fur is denser than normal fur and the guard hairs are about the same length as the undercoat. Rex fur also stands up perpendicular to the skin, giving it a unique feel.

4. The last type of fur is wool and is found on Angora rabbits. There are actually four different types of wool found on different types of Angoras.

For obvious reasons, Angoras require frequent brushing!

The care of an Angora coat is much different from that of other breeds because their wool—not fur—is quite long. For pet Angora rabbits, it is quite acceptable to keep their hair cut short so that it does not get as dirty and is easier to manage. If you do cut the fur, do not trim it right to the skin level. Fur offers natural protection against heat, cold, and anything that may injure the skin. Angoras will require frequent brushing, whereas other breeds of rabbits require less coat maintenance. It is especially important to *not* trim the fur from your rabbit's hocks and back feet, as this will definitely predispose him to hock sores.

Most rabbits, like cats, are fastidious groomers and will groom their coats to a nice, clean finish. Consequently, rabbits can end up swallowing a lot of hair and developing hairballs. To help reduce the amount of hair your rabbit will ingest, brush him at least once a week.

Shedding

If your rabbit is going through a heavy shed, you should brush him every day. Brushing should be done in the natural direction of the haircoat; if you reverse the stroke and go from tail to head too frequently, you will damage the hair.

Rabbits shed every three months. One shed will be light and may not even be noticeable; the next shed will be heavy. Rabbits can lose a lot of hair during a heavy shed and may even develop bald areas. It may be easier during these periods to gently pull out loose hair with your fingers and follow up with a brushing. Dampening your hands with water and stroking your rabbit from head to tail will also help remove dead hair.

Note: Each rabbit sheds for a different period of time. For some rabbits, the shed will only last a day or two; for others, it will last two weeks.

Brushes

Be careful when selecting a brush for your rabbit. Although rabbit coats are fairly thick, the skin underneath is very delicate and you obviously do not want to injure the skin with a painful brush. Also, you do not want your rabbit to feel discomfort or pain during your brushings—you want him to learn to enjoy brushings. For that reason, I do not think that slicker brushes and some hard metal brushes are appropriate. A bristle brush or pin brush is more appropriate for rabbit grooming.

Combing

To remove the most loose hair, you may want to follow a brushing with a combing. Use a fine-toothed comb so that it will grab the finer dead hairs. Some combs are silicone-coated to glide easily.

Tip: Long hair is very difficult to manage on rabbits. You should consider clipping the hair short, to about 1 inch (2.5 cm) in length.

Static Electricity

If you live in a dry climate, or if your house gets dry in the winter, be aware that your rabbit's hair may become flyaway from static electricity, as yours does. This may get worse with brushing and even precipitate small shocks as you touch your rabbit or as your rabbit moves on carpeting. You can imagine how disturbing that might be to a rabbit. Dampening the coat with water will help temporarily.

Mats

With proper grooming, your rabbit will be unlikely to develop fur mats, but they can happen, especially in rabbits that are not grooming themselves well or in rabbits with skin disease. *Never* cut a mat out with scissors; many small animal veterinarians see several patients a year to sew up lacerations caused by someone trying to cut a mat out. It is very difficult to tell where the mat ends and the skin begins: If the mat is small, it can be pulled out with a comb or a mat rake; if the mat is a bit larger, you can use the end of the comb to tease the mat apart and then comb it out. If you have a large section of matted fur, or cannot get a mat out, take your rabbit to a veterinarian or groomer to clip the mat out for you with electric clippers. You should be able to do this at home if you have fast-moving electric clippers. The lower-speed electric clippers do not work well on rabbits.

Bathing

In general, rabbits do not need to be bathed. For many rabbits, bathing is a stressful experience and, as a source of stress, it has the potential for bringing out illness. If your rabbit has only a small area of his body that needs to be cleaned, bathe that area only. Nonmedicated shampoos designed for dogs and cats are fine for rabbits. If you can find one, use a hypoallergenic non-soap shampoo with moisturizers or conditioners. *Do not use a shampoo made for humans;* our shampoos are very drying to animals. Make sure your rabbit does not become chilled from his bath. If necessary, rabbits can be dried with a hair dryer set to a warm setting. High settings should never be used because of the risk of heat stress.

If you absolutely must bathe your rabbit's face, be very sure to keep shampoo out of his eyes. If you are concerned that you may get water and shampoo into the eyes, you can protect them by applying a nonmedicated eye ointment over the cornea before the bath. A drop of mineral oil can be used as a substitute for eye ointment, but only use it sparingly.

Ears

When brushing your rabbit, check the ears to see if there is any wax buildup. Cotton swabs are the best and most gentle tools for removing the wax. If the wax is very dry or is tightly attached to the ear, you can soften it with a nonmedicated ear cleaner approved for cats, or with some mineral oil. It will be easy to remove once it has softened. Be careful not to push any of the wax down into the ear canal.

Nails

Check your rabbit's nails during your weekly brushing as well. If they are getting overgrown, clip them. If you are uncomfortable clipping the nails yourself, you may want to have a veterinary technician or groomer show you how to do it the first time.

If your rabbit has clear nails, you will be able to see where the "quick" is and where you should cut. The quick is the end of the live pink tissue in the nail bed and includes blood and nerves. If you cut this area, it will bleed and your rabbit will experience some pain. Cut the nail after the end of the quick, where you see only off-white nail, and no pink is left.

If your rabbit has dark nails, you will have to look more closely for the quick but you should still be able to find it. Sometimes you can see where the tissue ends if you look under the nail.

Have someone help you while you carefully trim your rabbit's nails.

If you do cut the quick and see bleeding, rub the nail across a bar of soap to seal the end. You can also purchase a styptic powder called Kwik Stop at pet stores to place on the bleeding nail. If you are uncomfortable trimming nails or if the sound frightens your rabbit, you can file the nails with an emery board or sandpaper instead.

Traveling

There will likely come a time when you plan to take a trip and your rabbit will not join you. A little advance planning ensures that you return to a rabbit that is as happy and healthy as when you left. If you will be gone for more than 24 hours, do not be tempted to leave your rabbit alone with extra food left for him; there is a very high risk of your rabbit eating improperly or becoming stressed and ill.

Leaving Your Rabbit Home

Your rabbit will do best if he stays in his own home and is fed the diet he is used to receiving. Of course, you will need someone to check on your rabbit every day, to provide fresh food and water, and be sure he is okay. Most people find it easiest to have a neighbor or friend help out; others hire a professional pet-sitter. Pet-sitters can be found through the phone book, your local rabbit society, or your veterinarian.

No matter who is entrusted with the care of your rabbit, be sure to go over with that caretaker all your expectations for your rabbit's care while you are gone. Do not assume that person will know exactly what to do without specific directions.

Food: To make things as simple for the sitter as possible, I recommend setting up daily rations of food in advance. Fresh fruits and vegetables can be cut up and stored in the refrigerator for about a week. Store the food in individual bags with a day marked on each; then all the pet-sitter has to do is take the day's food in its own bag and give it to the rabbit. Also show the sitter where the hay is kept and review how to rinse and refill the water bottle.

Care instructions: Even after showing the sitter what to do, make a detailed list of instructions.

• Include the feeding instructions, instructions for cleaning the rabbit hutch or litter box, and the phone number of your veterinarian.

• Review signs of illness with the sitter.

• Make arrangements for possible emergency care with your veterinarian in advance of your trip. With you gone, your veterinarian may be reluctant to pursue high-level diagnostics and treatment, but if you call in advance, your veterinarian will know that you have authorized care until you can be reached.

• Most important: Be sure to leave the sitter with a phone number where you can be reached every day of your trip. If it will be absolutely impossible to reach you, leave the number of someone you trust to make decisions in an emergency, but if you must leave someone else's number, be sure that person knows he or she may be put on the spot to make some decisions.

Leaving Your Rabbit at Someone Else's Home

If you cannot find someone to care for your rabbit in your own home, another option is to have your rabbit stay with a friend. The downside to that is that it may be more stressful for your rabbit to be in a different home, especially if there are other pets there with which your rabbit is not familiar. Do not leave your rabbit in a home with dogs that are likely to be predatory toward him, such as greyhounds or terriers.

Again, review all the instructions for the care of your rabbit in advance. Be sure that your friend is comfortable with these duties.

• When it is time to take your rabbit to your friend's home, be sure to include everything your rabbit will need. Bring a cage or hutch for him even if he does not usually use one at home; your friend's home is not likely to be as rabbit-proofed as yours and your friend may want to limit your rabbit at times.

• Bring your rabbit's litter box if he uses one, as well as any toys he is fond of.

• If your rabbit is shedding or is likely to shed while you are away, bring a grooming brush and be sure your friend knows how to brush your rabbit.

• Bring marked bags of prepared food for each day that you will be gone, as well as a water bottle.

• If your friend does not have a lot of rabbit experience, review the basic signs of illness in a rabbit—bring along this book for your friend to refer to.

• Leave the phone number of your veterinarian for emergencies as well as the number where you will be staying on your trip.

Boarding Your Rabbit

If you are unable to find someone trustworthy to visit your rabbit or stay with your rabbit in your home, you may need to board your rabbit at a kennel or veterinary hospital. This is certainly a better option than leaving your rabbit alone even for a couple of days when other options will not work.

Unfortunately, boarding can be very stressful for rabbits. Not only are they in a strange environment, but there will be cats and dogs present. Staff members at kennels and veterinary hospitals sometimes have limited experience with rabbits. Also, your rabbit is unlikely to get exercise outside his cage while kenneled.

Of the two, I would prefer a veterinary hospital to a boarding kennel for your rabbit. At the hospital your rabbit can be immediately examined and treated if anything happens during his stay. Before choosing the veterinary hospital as a temporary home, though, I would be sure there is a quiet room available for your rabbit away from the dogs. If you will be gone over a weekend, also check on what staffing is provided at the hospital when the hospital is closed.

If the staffing is extremely limited on weekends, or if the rabbit will be in a room with barking dogs, you may consider a kennel or cattery instead. Many boarding facilities have quieter rooms for cats and other noncanine pets. Boarding facilities also tend to have their fullest coverage on weekends and often have extended staff hours.

Traveling with Your Rabbit

In general, traveling with your rabbit is not a good option. All the changes travel brings are very stressful to a rabbit and predispose him to illness. Even something as simple as a difference in the drinking water can make your rabbit ill, and should your rabbit become ill while you are traveling, it may be difficult to find proper care.

If you are moving and must travel with your rabbit, you will certainly need these tips on safe traveling with your rabbit. If you are vacationing at someone's house, taking your rabbit may be an option. Make sure that your rabbit will be welcome and that no one in the house has allergies. If you are planning a very busy trip, it is best not to take your rabbit along.

Sedation: For car or plane travel, rabbits should never be sedated. They can have a variety of reactions to sedatives, ranging from no effect to a short effect to hours of grogginess. Also, sedatives reduce your rabbit's ability to handle changes in temperature or breathe properly if he is having difficulty. Pets that receive

A baby Rex stops for a snack.

sedatives for flying are more likely to die during a flight than pets that have not received sedatives.

Car travel: Get your rabbit used to car travel in advance by taking him on short rides with you before the trip.

• Rabbits should never be loose in the car.

• Place the rabbit's cage away from drafts from windows or air conditioning.

• A rubber mat under the cage will help keep the cage from moving during the car trip.

• *Never* leave a rabbit in a hot car—not even with the windows down or the air conditioning running. Rabbits are extremely susceptible to heatstroke and can die very quickly when overheated.

Carriers: Carriers specially made for rabbits are available through some pet outlets. If you cannot find a rabbit-specific carrier, a cage or kennel cab is a good alternative. The kennel cabs that are designed for dogs and cats do very well but are more difficult to keep clean because of their solid construction. Put an absorbent towel in the bottom. Bring extra towels for changes and a plastic bag for dirty towels. Choose a carrier or cage to which you can attach a water bottle and food bowl and try to position the carrier so that it will not slide during stops and turns.

Items to bring for your rabbit: Well in advance, gather all the items you will need to care for your rabbit during your trip. The last thing you need is to be running around trying to find a portable food dish just as you are trying to leave. Bring food, bottled water, a water bottle, food dishes, hay, towels, paper towels, plastic bags, a brush, and any medications your rabbit may need.

Health certificates: For travel by plane or outside the country, you will need a health certificate signed by a veterinarian. He or she will need to examine your rabbit to write a health certificate that states that the rabbit appears healthy enough to travel and appears to be free of any communicable diseases. As a general rule, the certificate must be dated within ten days of a flight within the United States. For flights to other countries, check the regulations of that country; generally, you will need an international health certificate signed and dated within 30 days of the flight. An international certificate must be signed by your veterinarian as well as by your state veterinarian. It is your responsibility to be sure that all the paperwork is in order before your trip.

Airlines: Airlines have for several years permitted small dogs, cats, and birds in the cabin. Airlines limit pets in the cabin by size—they must fit comfortably in a carrier that fits under the seat—and number—one or two permitted in the cabin for any flight. Many airlines do not permit rabbits in the cabin, but it is always worthwhile to check. If you are unable to find an airline that will let your rabbit fly with you in the cabin, he will be relegated to the baggage hold. There will be an extra fee whether your rabbit flies cargo or in the cabin, and an advance reservation for your pet is needed.

Some airlines provide a temperature-controlled hold for animals. Despite that, I would strongly discourage anyone from plane travel with a rabbit, especially if the rabbit would have to fly in cargo. The risk of overwhelming stress is quite high and you cannot guarantee how the crew will handle your rabbit or whether he will be exposed to extreme temperatures during loading and unloading. Your rabbit will also be subjected to extremely loud noises during loading and unloading, which will stress him.

Hotels: Many hotels will now accept small pets; call in advance to make sure the hotel you plan to stay at will allow your rabbit to stay there. There may be an extra charge for a pet in the room. Remember, we will all continue to be welcome at these hotels if we are good guests with our pets. This means making sure your rabbit is not destructive in the room. It is best to leave the rabbit in his cage and let him out only for exercise in the bathroom. Messes are easy to clean in the bathroom and there is no electrical cord or carpet

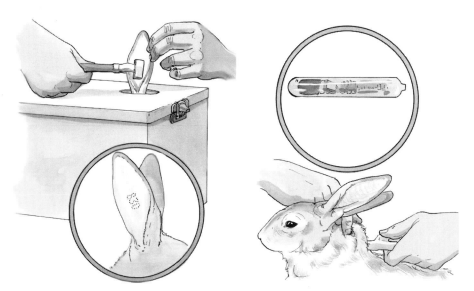

Rabbit breeders usually use ear tattooing for identification purposes, but microchip implants may be the wave of the future.

for your rabbit to chew on. If at all possible, be present in the room while it is being cleaned or take your rabbit out during cleaning. A strange person in this strange environment with cleaning equipment may add extra stress to your rabbit's day, and there is also a risk of the cleaning person letting your pet out.

Tattoos for Identification

Tattooing is a common means of identifying rabbits in the United States. It is usually performed around the time of weaning. The tattoo, placed in the rabbit's left ear, will be permanent and will not cause a disfiguration. Breeders make up their own system for the tattoos. Many breeders choose numbers, or a combination of

numbers and letters, that represent the birth date of the rabbit and which litter it was from. Some breeders include a code to indicate whether the rabbit is male or female. Because there is no universal system, rabbits cannot be tracked by their tattoos.

Another means of identifying rabbits is with a microchip. This chip is in a rice grain-sized container and is implanted between the shoulder blades of the pet. The chip can then be scanned if the pet arrives at a shelter or veterinary office. The number on the chip is registered to the owner so that the owner can be located. The implantation is quick and does not require anesthesia. Although the microchips have not been approved for use in any other species besides the dog and cat, there may come a time when rabbits are routinely chipped for identification.

Chapter Four
Nutrition

"Doc, I know you told me to give her the timothy hay, but she just won't touch it; she'll only eat the alfalfa. And she'll eat plenty of the dandelions but none of the other vegetables I want her to eat. I'll tell you, she's more stubborn than my three-year-old son when it comes to eating!"

Okay, so I cannot promise that your rabbit will eat all of the things we recommend in this section. Fortunately, your rabbit can live a long, healthy life even if he does not follow the best diet exactly. I do promise, however, that science and experience show that this balanced, nutritious diet gives your rabbit the best chance at staying healthy.

Rabbit Physiology

Rabbits choose to eat primarily in the early morning and at night. They have an interesting way of digesting their food. They are herbivorous monogastrics—plant eaters with one simple stomach. Many

These lucky rabbits are in vegetable heaven!

other plant eaters have complex stomachs or more than one stomach to help them digest their food.

Rabbits chew their food thoroughly, with up to 120 jaw movements per minute to start the digestive process. As the food moves through the stomach and intestines, it is digested and fermented. Rabbits have a very large cecum and lots of intestinal flora that are critical to the process. The bacteria in the cecum help produce essential vitamins and nutrients that your rabbit needs.

Some of these nutrients come out of the rabbit in special soft stools called cecotrophs. They are also called "night feces" and contain water, protein, and B vitamins that your rabbit needs. Rabbits eat this special stool directly from their anus once a day to take advantage of these nutrients. The name for this behavior is *coprophagy*. As horrid as this may seem to some pet owners, it is very important to your rabbit's health to do this. When you try to keep a rabbit from eating this stool or if your rabbit is impacted and not passing stool, he will become ill from missing these nutrients.

General Feeding Guidelines

Age/Condition	Diet
0–3 weeks	Mother's milk
3–4 weeks	Mother's milk and nibbles of alfalfa hay and pellets
4–7 weeks	Mother's milk and increased access to alfalfa hay and pellets
7 weeks–7 months	Unlimited amounts of alfalfa hay and pellets
12 weeks	Begin introducing vegetables one at a time
7 months–1 year	Start limiting access to pellets
	Begin decreasing the amount of alfalfa hay, substituting grass/timothy hay in its place
	Gradually increase the amount of vegetables offered
	Offer ½–1 ounce of fruit per 6 pounds (2.7 kg) of body weight
1–5 years	Unlimited grass hay
	¼–½ cup of pellets per 6 pounds (2.7 kg) body weight
	2+ cups of chopped vegetables
	About 1 ounce (28 g) of fruit per 6 pounds (2.7 kg)
Pregnant or lactating does	Feed an adult diet with alfalfa hay instead of grass hay and offer more pellets
	Offer food 24 hours a day
Cold weather	Offer more pellets and vegetables

The Basics
An adult rabbit that is not breeding should be fed:
• An unlimited amount of timothy hay
• ¼–½ cup of a high-quality rabbit pellet per day (for an average 6-pound [2.7-kg] rabbit)
• 2 or more cups of fresh vegetables a day
• 1 teaspoon of fresh fruit treats a day or less
Also, fresh water should always be available.

Hay

There are several types of hay. Each provides fiber, protein, vitamins, and minerals in varying amounts. Alfalfa hay has high levels of protein and calcium. It should be fed to growing rabbits that are less than a year old, breeding females, and rabbits that are not getting pellets. Most rabbits should be fed grass or timothy hay. It is lower in protein and calcium and higher in fiber.

Hay should always be offered free choice so that your rabbit can eat as much as he wants. A high-fiber content is critical to a rabbit's diet as it keeps the intestinal activity normal. The fiber that is in hay is much more effective than the fiber in pellets. When rabbits do not have enough fiber in their diet, they become overweight and develop intestinal problems and hairballs.

Choose leafy hay that does not have any mold. Store your hay so that it will not become moldy before you use it. If you live in the southwestern United States, be sure that you do not receive hay that may contain wooly pod milkweed, which is highly toxic to rabbits (see Milkweed Poisoning, page 65).

Pellets

Pellets are premixed, formed pieces of food. Several companies manufacture them for sale at pet stores and feed stores. Since pellets can spoil, try to purchase only six weeks' worth at a time. Although pellets contain as much as 23 percent fiber, rabbits still benefit from supplementation with hay.

Rabbits have a propensity to overeat their pellets and become obese. Because of that, you should limit how many pellets your rabbit gets each day when he is older than seven months. Between seven weeks and seven months, when

Pellet Feeding

Age	Amount
0–3 weeks	No pellets
3–4 weeks	Nibbles of pellets
4–7 weeks	Increased access to pellets
7 weeks–7 months	Unlimited access to pellets
7 months–1 year	Begin limiting pellets
1 year + (adults)	
5–7 pounds (2.3–3.2 kg)	¼–½ cup per day
8–10 pounds (3.6–4.5 kg)	about ½ cup per day
11–15 pounds (5–6.8 kg)	¾ cup per day

growth is rapid, your rabbit can eat as many pellets as he wants. Between seven months and one year, gradually decrease the amount of pellets he is eating so that by one year, he is getting ¼ to ½ cup of pellets for each 6 pounds (2.7 kg) of body weight.

Rabbits that weigh less than 2 pounds (.91 kg) may have a speedier metabolism than larger rabbits. Very small rabbits may have a higher need for energy and, as a result, less need for fiber. It may be appropriate to feed as much as ⅙ cup of pellets or more. You should judge the amount you feed by your rabbit's weight: feed more if he has difficulty maintaining weight, less if he tends to be overweight.

Fiber and protein: There is variation in commercial pelleted diets for rabbits, so spend some time comparing labels. The pellets will range from 12 to 25 percent crude fiber and 14 percent or higher crude protein. Pellets that have more than 18 percent fiber content are best; 20–25 percent fiber content is ideal. Choose a pellet with a protein level of 14–15 percent. A higher protein level of 16–22 percent is more appropriate if your rabbit lives outside. The calcium content should be less than 1 percent.

Animal proteins: Rabbits digest vegetable proteins very well, but not animal proteins. As in humans, animal fat can sometimes be problematic for rabbits. They have been known to develop atherosclerosis-like symptoms and cataracts when they are fed animal fat. Although this does not always occur, it is best to check pellet labels and minimize any animal products they are fed.

Fat: Rabbits have a very low fat requirement relative to other animals; they need their diet to contain only 2 percent fat. If the pellets you feed your rabbit have a much higher fat content, he will more likely become overweight.

Color: Some companies offer shaped or colored pellets. While that may be good marketing, you need to be sure it is also good nutrition for your rabbit. Always read the label to see what the food contains to be sure it does not contain too much fat, sugar, or animal products.

Size: A smaller pellet is best for young rabbits. Because of their small bite, they will eat a portion of a larger pellet and the remainder of the pellet often falls through the wire cage floor.

Pellet-only Diets

Some rabbitries feed only high-fiber alfalfa-based pellets. In my opinion, this is not the most ideal diet, but the places that do this feel that their rabbits remain quite healthy and do not have undue consequences from long-term feeding of these pellets. They do not routinely see the potential health problems from feeding a higher calcium alfalfa-based diet, perhaps because the pellets balance out the fiber, protein, and energy levels.

If you choose to feed a pellet-only diet, be sure not to change the type of pellets or suddenly add other foods to the diet. Any sudden diet change for a rabbit can have serious health consequences.

Vegetables

As another staple of the rabbit diet, the average 6-pound (2.7-kg) rabbit should eat 2 or more cups of fresh vegetables every day. It is best to feed a variety.

Carrot tops, carrots, broccoli, parsley, chicory, endive, and raddichio are all good choices. Dandelion greens are also healthy. Lettuce is another good choice as long as it is a dark leafy variety. Iceberg lettuce, on the other hand, is unsuitable. Avoid beans and potatoes.

Some vegetables, such as chard, spinach, and beet tops, are good only if they are fed in limited quantities—once or twice a week would be appropriate. If you feed too much of these, the oxalates in them accumulate in your rabbit and cause toxicity.

Because your rabbit will do best with a varied diet of greens, you might also try collecting some natural plants. Dandelions are an excellent source of nutrition for rabbits, as are plantains (common, English, or hoary). Coltsfoot, corn marigold, ragwort, and yarrow may also be fed. Do not pick plants from roadsides or from fields where pesticides may have been used.

Be sure to wash vegetables thoroughly before you offer them to your rabbit. Don't scrape or peel your carrots; instead, scrub them with a vegetable brush.

Treats

You may give your rabbit some special treats, but you should not offer more than a tablespoon full of treats per 5 pounds (2.3 kg) of body weight a day. Rabbits are very fond of sugary foods, but they can easily get too much of a good thing. Too much sugar, whether it is pure sugar or the sugar in fruits, can not only lead to obesity in your rabbit but may cause bacteria to overgrow in his gut. If this happens, more serious imbalances can occur. The intestines can stop working properly and your rabbit can then develop diarrhea and stop eating.

Acceptable treats in limited amounts are apple slices without seeds, pears, kiwi fruit, melon, and strawberries. Many other fruits and even fruit juices are okay. Some owners are tempted to offer their rabbits cookies or other refined carbohydrates. This is an extremely dangerous practice as it can lead to toxic bacterial overgrowth and excessive gas production.

Note: Fresh papaya juice, papaya extract, or pineapple juice is often recommended to help rid your rabbit of hairballs.

Water

It is absolutely critical that your rabbit have unlimited access to fresh water. Rabbits have a very great need for water compared to other animals. A rabbit will drink anywhere from 1¾ to 5 ounces of water a day for every 2.2 pounds (1 kg) of body weight. An average 6-pound (2.7-kg) rabbit will drink ½ to 2 cups of water per day. Of course, the amount your rabbit drinks will depend on the climate, how much water content is in his food, and his activity level.

When your rabbit is deprived of water, he will eat less food; withholding food will cause your rabbit to drink more water.

Water should be offered in a nonspill bottle. Check ball tips of water bottles frequently to make sure they are not sticking. Empty, rinse, and refill the bottle every day. Every week, disinfect the bottle with a dilute hypochlorite solution. Commonly, bleach is diluted by adding 40 parts water for each part bleach. This solution is used to disinfect water and food containers.

Warning: It is important to thoroughly rinse afterwards so that none of the bleach solution remains.

If your rabbit lives outdoors, be sure that the water does not freeze or your rabbit will not get any water at all.

Dietary Adjustments

As we have mentioned, it is extremely important that any changes in your rabbit's diet be made gradually. This is even more critical for rabbits between 4 and 12 weeks of age. Whether you are introducing a new food or changing the quantities of different foods you feed your rabbit, make the change over four or more days. For example, if you want to introduce romaine lettuce to your rabbit, give only a 50-cent-piece-sized leaf on the first day. Double the amount every day thereafter until you are feeding as much as you want to in order to balance your rabbit's diet.

When you make changes too quickly, you change the rabbit's intestinal environment including the pH, the osmolarity, and the types of starches present. When this happens quickly, your rabbit can have dramatic changes in intestinal flora, the bacteria and organisms that help him digest his food. That can be toxic. If you allow the flora to change slowly, with gradual diet changes, the problems will not occur.

If you are trying to switch your rabbit from alfalfa hay to grass hay, and he goes on a hunger strike rather than eat the timothy, there are a couple of techniques you can try:

1. Gradually decrease the amount of alfalfa hay and slowly increase the timothy hay; or

2. Reduce the amount of pellets and ration them. If you offer only a reduced number of pellets twice a day and a normal amount of vegetables, your rabbit should be hungry enough between meals to eat the grass hay.

Restricting Food

If a rabbit is restricted from eating appropriate amounts, it can exhibit many deleterious side effects such as pulling its fur or gnawing on carpets and furniture. If you are always providing grass hay and a variety of fresh vegetables, these problems will not occur.

Chapter Five

Medical Care

Rabbits do not always show you when they are ill; sometimes, they have very advanced disease before they show obvious symptoms, so you must pay attention to subtle cues that your rabbit may be giving you. Something as simple as having less energy or having a discharge from the nose can be a symptom of a more serious underlying problem.

This chapter covers general medical advice for the pet rabbit owner. It also covers the major medical problems of pet rabbits housed in the United States. Some of them are common; some are very rare. If you familiarize yourself with the symptoms of some of these disorders, you will be able to take better care of your rabbit and know when to seek professional veterinary care.

You can also use this reference to narrow down a problem your rabbit may be having so that you will know what to expect when you get your pet to the veterinarian's office. Finally, use this section to read up on any disease or disorder your rab-

bit has been diagnosed with. It will help you understand his treatment better and allow you to have a more educated discussion with your veterinarian about the problem. Do not hesitate to ask your veterinarian any questions.

Warning: I would like to caution you not to attempt to diagnose a medical problem in your rabbit without the help of your veterinarian—sometimes, information can get you into trouble. On the one hand, you can start to get paranoid that there are a lot of things wrong with your rabbit simply because he is having a bad day. Perhaps he is a little warm and does not want to move around much; all of a sudden, you may be making a diagnosis of everything from pneumonia to cancer. On the other hand, if you already believe you have diagnosed the problem, you may find it more difficult to work with your veterinarian, who may be telling you the problem is something else. So, keep an open mind, gather all the information you can, and rely on your veterinarian as a partner in the care of your pet.

Taking Your Rabbit to the Veterinarian

Traveling can be a stressful experience for your rabbit; he does not do it very often and has no idea what is happening. You don't want your rabbit to get anxious and injure himself trying to jump out of your arms or around a moving car. Place some newspaper or a towel along with some food in the bottom of the carrier. Bring a towel with you for the metal examining table at the veterinarian's office; it is slippery and cold to a rabbit. A rabbit will be more comfortable and easier to examine on a towel or small blanket. If your rabbit has a significant illness, the veterinarian may need to keep him for testing or treatment. If there is any chance of that happening, bring a couple of days' worth of your rabbit's food and his water sipper bottle. This will save you a trip back and forth. Veterinarians rarely keep rabbit food in stock.

Talking to Your Veterinarian

If you do need to take your rabbit to the veterinarian for an evaluation, you will be able to help him or her diagnose the problem if you come prepared with certain information. Your veterinarian should know:
• the conditions under which the rabbit is kept—indoors or out, in a cage, or with free run of the house
• how your rabbit is fed and with what specific foods
• when your rabbit last ate
• what your rabbit's urine and stool production have been
• anything your rabbit could have been exposed to
• what symptoms you have been noticing

Do not be upset if your veterinarian picks up on something that you missed; that is the doctor's job.

First Aid Kit

What a blessing it would be if your rabbit lived to a ripe old age without a single health problem requiring your attention. Unfortunately, that is rarely the case. Whether your rabbit is exposed to harmful bacteria, eats the wrong food, gets overheated, or chews on an electrical cord, there will likely be a time you need to be prepared to offer care to him. To help you be prepared, I recommend that you keep a kit with the following items:
• a *digital* thermometer (not glass), to be used rectally
• 6 or 12 cc syringe without a needle
• hot water bottle
• antibacterial cleanser, preferably chlorhexiderm or betadine/iodine-based
• eyewash; you can use eyewash made for humans or the sterile saline solution used by contact lens wearers
• sterile gauze
• Poison Control hotline phone number
• your veterinarian's phone number and the emergency clinic's phone number

Note: A normal rectal temperature for a rabbit is anywhere between 101 and 104°F (38–40°C). The temperature will be only as high as 104°F and still normal if your rabbit is stressed but not overheated. For example, some rabbits will have rectal temperatures between 102 and 104°F (39–40°C) when they are brought to the veterinary hospital. If the temperature is 104°F or greater, and there is a chance of overheating or heat stress, it is a sign of a problem.

Pain

It can be difficult to tell if your rabbit is in pain; he cannot scream and cry like we can. The following can be signs of pain as well as signs of illness:
• limp or change in gait
• abnormal posture, such as hunching the back
• licking, rubbing, or scratching an area
• anorexia (lack of appetite)
• grinding teeth
• faster or heavier breathing
• inability to sleep
• decreased activity and movement
You should *never* treat your rabbit with any pain medications that have not been approved by your veterinarian. Of course, it is always important to determine what is causing the pain.

Emergencies

Because emergencies do not always occur during regular business hours, you should know in advance how to reach a veterinarian after hours. Your own veterinarian may take his or her own emergency calls or may refer calls to a local emergency clinic. If an emergency clinic is used, call to make sure they see rabbits. Most emergency hospitals do.

The following are life-threatening situations that require immediate attention:
• unresponsiveness/coma
• seizures
• head tilt or falling to the side
• severe or ongoing bleeding
• heatstroke (see page 60)
• low body temperature—below 99°F (37.2°C)
These situations are very serious and should also be dealt with immediately:
• animal attacks
• maggots (see page 62)
• respiratory problems
• severe diarrhea
• constipation
A normal heart rate for a rabbit varies tremendously, depending on the individual rabbit and whether he is at rest or active or anxious. The rate can be anywhere between 130 and 325 beats per minute. The normal respiratory rate for a rabbit (how many breaths it takes) is 30 to 60 per minute.

Poisons
Because rabbits have a habit of getting into things and eating things we wish they would not, your rabbit may eat something toxic—a cleaner you are using or a houseplant. If you believe your rabbit ate something

that is potentially toxic, call your veterinarian and poison control hotline right away. (See page 131 for phone number.)

The Poison Control Center will be able to tell you whether the item your rabbit was exposed to is poisonous. If it has toxic properties, the people there will tell you how it needs to be treated and will consult with your veterinarian about the treatment for no additional charge. The center has contracts with companies that make certain pesticides and cleaners. If your pet has been exposed to a product from those companies, there will not be any charge for the consultation.

Medicating Your Rabbit

Rabbits do not know what is good for them. Sometimes we need to

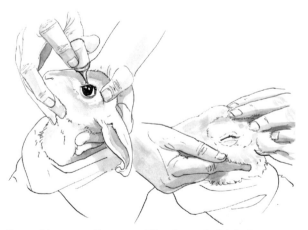

Try and be as gentle as possible when administering eyedrops to your rabbit.

gently, but firmly, make sure that a rabbit gets the treatments he needs, which often means being smarter at getting medications into the rabbit than he is at getting them out.

Generally, I find it helpful to prepare in advance to medicate or treat the rabbit. Gather together any medications and equipment you need. Clear an area to sit with the rabbit or an area on the table to use. I find it easiest to wrap the rabbit in a towel for eye medications or oral medications if he tends to be fidgety.

Eyedrops

1. Remove the cap from the medication before starting.

2. Place the rabbit in your lap.

3. Gently hold the rabbit's head in one hand and lift his head until his eyes are looking up.

4. Use your finger on the same hand to gently hold the eyelid open.

5. Pick up the medication with your free hand and, from several inches above the eye, drop the liquid into the eye. Do not touch the tip of the bottle to the rabbit's tissues; it will contaminate the container.

Eye Ointment

1. Place the rabbit in your lap facing out.

2. Use one hand to gently lift the upper eyelid so that the white part of the eye shows.

3. With the other hand, squeeze a small amount of the ointment—as described by your veterinarian—onto this area. The upper eyelid can be used to cut the stream of ointment.

Nursing a rabbit back to health can be a good lesson for children.

4. It is very important that you not poke the eye with the tube of medication. Try very hard not to touch the tip of the medicine to the eye to prevent it from becoming contaminated as well. It is not necessary to rub the ointment around the eye.

Giving Pills or Liquids by Mouth

Again, always be sure to have everything you need before starting. With some liquid and tablet medications, rabbits will actually take them and swallow them just because they are put in front of them. Liquids can always be mixed with your rabbit's favorite food to get him to eat them, or perhaps mixed with a small

amount of applesauce or fruit-flavored (especially strawberry) yogurt. Just check with your veterinarian that it is safe to mix the medication. You might also request an extra couple of doses so that you can experiment with ways to convince your rabbit to eat it. Pills can often be crushed and mixed with food in a similar manner.

If your rabbit is not eating well, or will not take the medications in food, you will have to put the medicine in the rabbit's mouth. For a liquid medication:

1. Place the rabbit in your lap facing away or safely wrapped on a table.

2. Gently insert the dropper or syringe between the lips and over the rabbit's tongue.

3. Point the dropper or syringe to the back of the mouth and slowly squirt all the medication in. If you get some of the medicine on the rabbit's face, clean it thoroughly with a damp cloth so that it does not damage the skin.

To give your rabbit a pill:

1. Use one hand to open the mouth.

2. Place a finger at the edges of each side of the mouth and lift the top of the mouth up. Use your other finger to place the pill at the back of the tongue.

3. Hold the rabbit's mouth closed until he has swallowed the pill. This technique can be very trying. An alternative is to crush the pill and mix it with some water or mix it with some food into a slurry. You can then use a dropper or syringe to give the pill as a liquid medicine.

If you are finding it simply impossible to medicate your rabbit, do not give up and stop medicating. Get help from a friend with rabbit experi-

ence, or check with your veterinarian to see if you can take your rabbit in for injections of the medication instead.

Syringe Feeding

If your rabbit is not eating properly, you will have to force-feed him. His pellets can be mixed with water and some yogurt into a slurry in a blender or food processor. The slurry can then be pulled up into a syringe and force-fed to the rabbit. Because you will be putting the syringe in the rabbit's mouth many times a day, you need to be sure that you are careful and do not traumatize the mouth. You should follow the procedure described above for giving liquid medications by syringe.

Antibiotics

These bacteria-stopping agents are often necessary to combat illness in rabbits; however, rabbits are very sensitive to certain antibiotics and their use can have serious consequences. If your veterinarian decides that your rabbit needs to be on antibiotics, you should discuss with him or her how to prevent complications.

The antibiotics to be most concerned about in rabbits are: amoxicillin, amoxicillin-clavulinic acid, ampicillin, cephalosporins, clindamycin, erythromycin, lincomycin, and penicillin. These are all generic names and classes of drugs. If you are not sure if the antibiotic you are using falls into one of these categories, ask your veterinarian. The reason these antibiotics can be espe-

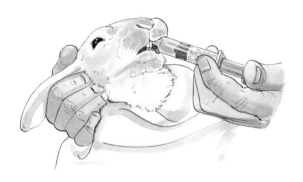

It's important to be careful while syringe feeding your rabbit.

cially problematic is that they kill some of the rabbit's normal intestinal flora in addition to the bacteria they should be killing. In simple terms, when all the good and normal bugs don't populate the gut, pathogens, or bad bugs, can take their place. When pathogens are present, the rabbit can develop enteritis and become toxic. Some rabbits have died as a result.

As a general rule, if your rabbit needs to be placed on antibiotics, he should also be given yogurt, which has live acidophilus cultures that replace some of the good gut bugs, the normal flora. Ideally, the yogurt should be started before the antibiotics. Increasing your rabbit's fiber consumption may also help.

Specific Medical Problems

Abscesses

Abscesses are pockets of infection. They can be found anywhere in the body but often appear as non-painful bumps just under the skin. A rabbit that is carrying Pasteurella multocida bacteria can spontaneously develop a pocket of infection due to the bacteria. Abscesses will also occur where there has been some injury or damage to the skin. Abscesses in rabbits often contain a common skin bacteria, Staphylococcus aureus, as well as other bacterial pathogens. Some rabbits develop abscesses behind the eye that can cause pain and bulging of the eye.

In other animals, the purulent material in abscesses—commonly called pus—is a thick fluid and contains bacteria as well as some blood and many white blood cells that are trying to fight off the bacterial infection. In rabbits, the purulent material tends to be thicker than it is in other animals. The lumps will feel more solid.

If you suspect that your rabbit has an abscess, you must take him to your veterinarian, who will attempt to determine the cause of the abscess to see if future abscesses can be prevented. The veterinarian will also start your rabbit on antibiotics to help fight off the infection. If the abscess is small, your veterinarian may recommend removing the entire abscess with surgery. If it is larger, he or she will more likely open up the abscess and drain the matter, teaching you how to continue to drain it at home.

Symptoms: Lumps in the skin or under the skin

Cause: Pasteurella bacteria chronically carried in the body, trauma to the skin

Treatment: Remove or drain abscess; antibiotics

Prevention: Good husbandry to keep your rabbit's skin healthy and his environment clean; purchase a rabbit without a history of exposure to Pasteurella

Coccidia

Coccidia are microscopic parasites that are often found in the intestines of many types of animals.

They are the most common parasites of rabbits and can make rabbits ill. Coccidia are present in many rabbitries. Infection is minimized in rabbitries by giving the rabbits medication to kill the coccidia.

One type of coccidia, *Eimeria stiedae,* live in the liver of rabbits. In mild infestations, the only symptom may be poor growth. Heavy infestations can cause death because the coccidia interfere with the normal function of the liver. A veterinarian may note that the rabbit's liver feels enlarged. Your veterinarian can look at your rabbit's stool to isolate the coccidia. To do that, the stool must be floated in a special solution and the veterinarian must look for the coccidia under the microscope.

All other types of coccidia are intestinal. Most infections will cause no symptoms; however, in young rabbits that are infected, you may see weight loss and diarrhea.

Symptoms: None, diarrhea, poor growth, anorexia

Cause: Coccidia passed from the stool of infected rabbits

Treatment: Medication such as trimethoprim-sulfa drugs to kill the coccidia

Prevention: Good hygiene; remove infected feces

Diarrhea

Diarrhea is not a disease itself; rather, it is a symptom of disease. Technically, soft stools cannot be called diarrhea, although they can still be a symptom of a problem. With diarrhea, your rabbit will have more frequent bowel movements or very loose bowel movements. Sometimes, the stool will actually be watery and may even contain blood or mucus.

Diarrhea is a symptom of an intestinal disorder. Along with other symptoms your rabbit is showing, it will help your veterinarian determine the cause. Soft, clumping stools can be a symptom of a high-carbohydrate, low-fiber diet, a sign of stress, or a sign of more advanced intestinal disease.

In rabbits between the ages of 1 and 14 days, diarrhea is usually caused by Escherischia coli bacteria in the intestines. It will affect the entire litter and is usually fatal. In weanling rabbits, diarrhea is often caused by bacterial enteritis. In adult rabbits, diarrhea can be caused by enteritis, enterotoxemia, foreign bodies including hairballs, and changes in diet.

Rabbits can also carry and be exposed to viruses that can cause diarrhea. This is much more of an issue where rabbits are being raised in groups. A coronavirus, for example, can occasionally be isolated from normal adults. If young, weanling rabbits are exposed to the coronavirus, they will develop diarrhea, lethargy, and abdominal swelling. Almost 100 percent of them will die within 24 hours of the beginning of symptoms. A rotavirus can also be a cause of diarrhea in young rabbits. Fortunately, the death rate with this virus is not as high.

Symptoms: Loose or more frequent stools.

Cause: Anything that irritates the intestines

Treatment: Treat the specific cause of the diarrhea; provide supportive care

Prevention: Good husbandry, proper diet, gradual diet changes

Ear Mites

Ear mites are caused by a contagious, microscopic, spiderlike bug. A rabbit with ear mites will have a lot of crusty material in his outer ears. The ear mites that infest rabbits' ears are called *Psoroptes cuniculi.* It is not the same type of mite that cats and dogs commonly get. Cats have been known to carry the *Psoroptes* mite and pass it on to rabbits.

Rabbits with ear mites often scratch at their ears and shake their heads. A simple infestation caught early may be treated by cleaning the discharge from the outer ears and applying mineral oil. More complicated cases need to be treated with medication, usually ivermectin, dispensed by your veterinarian.

Symptoms: Flaky discharge in the ears, scratching at the ears

Cause: Psoroptes cuniculi mite from another infected rabbit

Treatment: Mineral oil applied to the ear; medication from your veterinarian

Prevention: Keep infested rabbits away from other rabbits

Encephalitozoonosis

Encephalitozoon cuniculi is a parasite found in rabbits throughout the world. Does can pass it on to their young. Rabbits can also get it when it is shed in the urine of infected rabbits. The parasite goes to the kidneys and brain. It does not cause obvious disease in the kidneys, but in the brain, infection can cause a head tilt, loss of use of the hind legs, or an unsteady gait.

Some infected rabbits will never show signs of the infection. Rabbits that do have symptoms should be provided with supportive care. There is no specific treatment to kill the parasite. Infected rabbits should be kept away from other rabbits. A blood test can be performed to see which rabbits are infected.

Symptoms: Loss of use of back legs, urine scald, head tilt, unsteadiness

Cause: Encephalitozoon cuniculi parasite

Treatment: Supportive care; no specific treatment

Prevention: Isolate infected rabbits; prevent infected does from breeding

Enteritis

Enteritis is an inflammation or infection of the intestines that has many causes. It is one of the leading causes of death in weanling rabbits, causing 12 to 15 percent of deaths in 30- to 72-day-old rabbits. Rabbits under 2.1 ounces (60 g) are also highly susceptible, as are rabbits receiving certain antibiotics. This is one of the most common of all rabbit diseases.

Enteritis is caused by a sequence of events. A number of problems can start the sequence, among them improper feeding of weanling rabbits. These young rabbits are not yet fully capable of digestion. If they receive too many carbohydrates early on from a sudden change to a growth diet, many of the starches or carbohydrates will reach the large intestine before they have been digested. Another sequence starter is the administration of antibiotics, particularly penicillin, ampicillin, and lincomycin, which kill off certain types of bacteria in the gut. As a result of either of these circumstances, undesirable bacteria such as Clostridium spiroforme or Bacillus piliformis begin to overgrow.

Once the bacteria overgrow, they cause toxic side effects and diarrhea. You may see abnormal stools for months from enteritis or, on the other end of the spectrum, it can be severe enough to kill your rabbit within 24 hours. Other events that can lead to enteritis are too much food, the wrong types of food, stress, poorly moving (hypomotile) intestines, or genes (heredity) that predispose the rabbit to enteritis.

Proper feeding is one of the keys to preventing enteritis. Remember that any diet change should always be made gradually. Be sure that your rabbit is getting a diet with fiber levels between 18 and 23 percent. Weanlings should be started on a high-fiber diet and gradually switched, over two weeks, to a growth diet. A doe that has just delivered should have the amount of food she is offered gradually increased. If your rabbit needs to be placed on antibiotics, a higher-fiber diet and yogurt started before the antibiotics have been known to increase the survival rate.

Symptoms: Anorexia, listlessness, rough haircoat, bloat, weight loss, increased water consumption, teeth grinding, changing or intermittent diarrhea

Cause: Improper diet, stress, genetics, bacteria, slow-moving intestines; usually many of these factors play a part

Treatment: Under veterinary care, fluids, an antidiarrheal and perhaps an antibacterial such as neomycin or Chloramphenicol. Increasing the fiber in the diet is also critically important.

Prevention: Choose a rabbit from healthy stock; provide good husbandry; feed your rabbit properly; strictly adhere to good sanitation practices; have wire floor cages in your hutch

Enterotoxemia

Enterotoxemia is enteritis intensified. It is the same as the enteritis described above except that there is a severe change in the gut environment causing dangerous iota-like toxins. As with enteritis, newly weaned rabbits are at highest risk.

A rabbit with enterotoxemia quickly stops eating and becomes depressed. He will have watery, brown diarrhea that sometimes has mucus or blood in it. Death can occur within two days. In a few cases, the rabbit does not die but will continue to have the disease and have weight loss, periods of poor appetite, and diarrhea.

Symptoms: Anorexia, diarrhea

Cause: Toxins produced by pathogenic flora (overgrowth of harmful bacteria) in the intestines

Treatment: Supportive care; fluids; antibiotics; high-fiber diet

Prevention: Minimize stress; wean appropriately (do not force); high-fiber diet; no sudden diet changes

Fleas

These are the same pesky little critters that you might find on your dog or cat. Even an indoor rabbit can get fleas if you have another pet that brings them inside or if you have an infestation in your house. Sometimes it is very difficult to find fast-moving fleas on your pet unless a large number are present.

To check for fleas, I recommend rubbing the coat backwards to look at the skin, and checking the underside of your rabbit. Fleas are small, about the size of a grain of rice, and range from brown to black in color.

Flea sprays and powders that are considered safe for cats are also considered safe for rabbits. The new once-a-month spot-ons that are being used for cats have not been tested on rabbits. Although the ingredients in these spot-ons for cats are very safe, I cannot recommend them for rabbits until more information is available. For small numbers of fleas, you may also use a flea comb to comb the fleas out and kill them.

Whenever you have fleas on pets that come indoors, you will also have fleas living in your home—whether you see them or not. Always be sure to treat the home with pyrethrin-based premise sprays or insect growth regulators, along with every pet in the house.

Symptoms: Itching, visible fleas

Cause: Exposure to fleas from outside, other pets, infested environment

Treatment: Flea-control spray or powder labeled safe for cats (use sparingly)

Prevention: Keep rabbit out of infested areas; keep him away from other animals carrying fleas; use safe flea spray as a preventive if at risk

Foreign Bodies

A foreign body is anything that is inside your rabbit's body that should not be there. Usually it is a hairball, but it can be just about anything—rabbits commonly eat carpet fibers or pieces of plastic.

Foreign bodies do not always keep moving. They can be small enough for your rabbit to swallow but too large to pass the stomach or intestines, which causes an obstruction or irritation allowing nothing else to get past it.

A rabbit with a troublesome foreign body will often shows signs of abdominal pain. He will stop eating and stop producing stools. If an obstructing foreign body is not removed immediately, the rabbit will die.

Your veterinarian will examine your rabbit and take radiographs. If the veterinarian sees signs of a foreign body, he or she will perform surgery to remove it and remove any damaged tissue.

Symptoms: Abdominal pain, loss of appetite, lack of stools

Cause: Ingesting something inappropriate

Treatment: Usually surgery, if not a hairball

Prevention: Rabbit-proofing the environment

Fur Mites

Mites are tiny spiderlike bugs. Different types of mites live on different places on the body. Most mites are contagious among animals of the same species and across species; the rabbit fur mite is no exception. That means that the rabbit fur mite is contagious from one rabbit to another and can be spread to other animals and humans.

The rabbit fur mite is called *Cheyletiella parasitovorax.* It is commonly seen in southern California. Some rabbits will have such mild symptoms from the mite that you may not know they have it, while other rabbits will get dandruff and dry skin. The most affected rabbits will start to lose hair and have inflamed, scaly skin. They may also itch.

A veterinarian can diagnose fur mites by scraping a rabbit's skin or doing a tape preparation and looking at it under the microscope. Once diagnosed, your veterinarian will treat your rabbit with a special medicated dip or injections of ivermectin to kill the mites.

Symptoms: Dandruff, dry skin, hair loss, scaly skin, itching

Cause: Cheyletiella parasitovorax mite

Treatment: Dips; injections

Prevention: Keep infected animals away from all other animals

Hairballs/Trichobezoars

Trichobezoar is the 50-cent medical word for a hairball. Rabbits ingest shed hair in their environment or loose hairs off their bodies as they groom. The hair then groups together in the stomach to form a clump or ball.

Many people with cats are familiar with hairballs, especially if their cats are diligent groomers. When a cat gets a large amount of hair built up in its stomach, the cat will vomit it up. We try to prevent that by giving the cat hairball laxatives to move the hair through the gastrointestinal tract before it becomes a problem.

The difference with rabbits is that they are unable to vomit, so they can get in the difficult position of having a troublesome hairball and no easy way to get it out. This is also called "wool block" in rabbits. Rabbits are more likely to have problems with hairballs if they are on a high-carbohydrate, low-fiber diet, which slows down movement in the gastrointestinal tract. Limited exercise and stress also predispose your rabbit to having a hairball by slowing things down. If the GI tract is moving slowly, the hair will accumulate faster into a ball and quickly become a troublesome size. Keep in mind that rabbits shed about every three months and alternate a heavy shed with a light shed. The opportunity for hairballs increases during the shedding period.

If a hairball is stuck in the rabbit's stomach and does not pass through, you may notice a number of symptoms. The rabbit will most likely eat less, drink more, have fewer feces, and lose weight. This can continue to progress until the rabbit dies. Nothing can pass a large hairball stuck at the end of the stomach in the pyloric region.

As you can see, hairballs can be a very serious problem. If you are suspicious that your rabbit may have a hairball, take him immediately to your veterinarian, who may take radiographs to look for the hairball. If the veterinarian confirms the hairball, medical or surgical treatment may be recommended. If he or she determines that medical treatment is appropriate at first, your rabbit will likely be treated with a combination of treatments including mineral oil, metoclopramide, which is a drug to move things through the gastrointestinal tract, extra fluids, fresh pineapple juice, and increased dietary fiber. If the condition is too severe, your veterinarian will recommend surgery to remove the hairball. Unfortunately, the risk of surgery may be increased in rabbits with hairballs because of their poor condition and stomach damage prior to surgery.

Symptoms: May have no symptoms or anorexia, progressive weight loss, increased water consumption, fewer feces

Cause: Excessively eating hair, lack of fiber, boredom, stress, obesity

Treatment: Medical treatment with fiber and pineapple juice along with medications; surgical removal of the hairball

Prevention: Low-stress environment; high-fiber diet; an enriching environment to promote activity; regular hair clips for Angora rabbits; brushing your rabbit during his shed

Hair Loss

There are many things that can cause your rabbit to lose hair, some of which relate to the normal behaviors of rabbits and not to a medical disorder.

Dominant rabbits may actually pull out the hair of subordinate rabbits. The subordinate rabbits will have plucked or broken hairs on their heads and backs. These rabbits will need to be separated to prevent this barbering. Pregnant does will pull their own hair from their undersides to build a nest as delivery nears.

Some rabbits on low-fiber diets have also been reported to pull their hair. Other causes of hair loss are fur mites, ringworm, wounds, and infections.

Symptoms: Thinning hair, patches of lost hair

Cause: Behavioral reasons, mites, ringworm, wounds

Treatment: Depends on specific cause

Prevention: Good husbandry and health care

Head Tilt

Head tilt in rabbits can vary from a bit of a tilt to one side to a dramatic twisting of the entire head and neck all the way to the ground. This condition is also called torticollis or wry neck. The most common cause in standard breeds of rabbits is a middle ear infected by Pasteurella multocida. In dwarf breeds, head tilt is often caused by the parasite *Encephalitozoon cuniculi* invading the brain. Head tilt can also be caused by injuries to the head.

All of these disorders damage nerves. When the vestibular nerve is affected, the rabbit no longer knows which way is up. That causes the rabbit to turn its head to one side. Sometimes, the cause of the head tilt can be treated, and sometimes not. Your veterinarian will need to determine what is causing the head tilt and begin treatment.

Symptoms: Head tilt to one side, neck twist to one side

Cause: Trauma, Pasteurella, *Encephalitozoon*

Treatment: Depends on cause

Prevention: Keep rabbits free of Pasteurella and *Encephalitozoon;* prevent traumatic injuries

Heatstroke

Heatstroke occurs when the body becomes overheated and can no longer control its own temperature. As the body temperature rises, it reaches a critical level where the body can no longer function and death follows. Because animals as a rule do not perspire, they are at greater risk for heatstroke than we are. They regulate their body temperature through drinking water and breathing harder to blow off the heat. Some animals have a limited ability to perspire or blow off heat in other ways; for example, rabbits can blow off heat through their ears. Despite that, rabbits are especially susceptible to heatstroke. Temperatures over 85°F (29.4°C) are potentially dangerous.

A rabbit with heatstroke will have a body temperature of 102°F (38.9°C) or higher. The prognosis for recovery is poor. If you believe your rabbit is overheated, immediately immerse his body in cool, but not icy, water—it is dangerous to bring the temperature down too quickly. Be careful not to let the rabbit's head get in the water. Take him to your veterinarian to be treated with IV fluids and medications.

To make sure your rabbit does not get heatstroke, try to limit his exposure to the heat and direct sun. Provide shade and plenty of water. Some people put ice packs in the hutch as well.

Symptoms: Heavy breathing, lack of movement, elevated body temperature

Cause: Overheating

Treatment: Apply cool water (not icy); IV fluids

Prevention: Provide plenty of cool water and shade

Hepatic Lipidosis

Hepatic refers to the liver; lipids are fats; therefore, as you might guess, hepatic lipidosis is a fatty liver. When a rabbit does not get enough food, it tries to use its body stores to feed itself, but unfortunately, the body does not always process things properly. Rabbits can deposit the fat they are metabolizing abnormally in the liver. When that happens, the liver can no longer function properly and the rabbit gets even sicker.

This problem will often go undiagnosed unless your rabbit has abdominal surgery. Sometimes, the problem will show up in blood tests.

To treat hepatic lipidosis, you need to have the veterinarian treat the original problem, the one that caused the rabbit to stop getting enough nutrition. In addition, the rabbit should be IV-fed or force-fed food and fluids, to help it recover.

Symptoms: Anorexia, loose stools
Cause: Anorexia or limited nutrition
Treatment: Treat the underlying problem; force-feed
Prevention: Always provide adequate nutrition and treat any causes of decreased appetite aggressively

Intestinal Worms

Like dogs and cats, rabbits can carry worms in their intestines, but unlike dogs and cats, the worms very rarely cause a problem. Rabbits commonly have a pinworm called *Passalurus ambiguus.* Sometimes, worms are seen in fresh feces. Rabbits that eat fresh grass may also have *Obelis-* *coides cuniculi* in their intestines. These should not be seen in the feces; only their eggs can be seen in the feces by using a microscope. It would be unusual for either worm to cause a problem for your rabbit, but both can be easily treated with medication from your veterinarian.

There are other worms that wild rabbits are exposed to, some of which, such as flukes, can cause problems. However, unless your rabbit is frequenting wet meadows and the like, you should not worry about these other worms.

Symptoms: Usually none
Cause: Ingestion of parasitic eggs
Treatment: Dewormers such as thiabendazole, fenbendazole, and ivermectin
Prevention: Clean environment; no exposure to wet grasses

Kidney Disease

Rabbits can have kidney problems for many reasons. Sometimes, they have a genetic condition causing multiple cysts in the kidneys; sometimes, kidney disease is caused by bacteria that infect the kidneys or by medications the rabbit has been given. It is also caused by excess calcium in the diet.

The signs of kidney disease often depend on how severe the disease is: The more severe the disease, the worse the symptoms, which would include excessive drinking and urinating, urine burn on the perineum, loss of appetite, and lethargy.

A veterinarian will diagnose kidney problems after getting a blood

Be sure to inspect new rabbits for signs of disease before taking them home.

sample and a urine sample from the rabbit. The treatment depends on the exact cause of the kidney disease, but always includes giving the rabbit fluids to flush out his system. Many cases of kidney disease are so severe that the kidneys cease functioning altogether. In this situation, your veterinarian may be able to help control your rabbit's symptoms for a period of time, but ultimately, your rabbit will die from the kidney disease if it is that advanced.

Symptoms: Excessive drinking and urinating, urine scald, anorexia, lethargy

Cause: High-calcium diet, bacterial infection, cysts, medications

Treatment: Fluids to diurese; diet change; antibiotics

Prevention: Choose a rabbit from a line that has no history of polycystic kidneys (renal cysts); feed a diet with an appropriate calcium content; avoid medications such as gentamicin that may be damaging to the kidneys

Maggots, Fly Strike (see also Myiasis)

In a word, gross. I have seen even the bravest veterinary technicians falter or leave the room when a severe maggot infestation arrived at the hospital. Maggots, quite simply, are fly larvae. Flies land on the rabbit and try to find an irritated or diseased spot of skin. They like to choose this spot on which to lay their eggs so their offspring will have something to eat as they grow. The eggs grow into larvae that start out tiny and off-white, and grow to be large (several millimeters) and off-white. The larvae move a lot and eat into even the healthy tissue of the rabbit, on the skin and below, wreaking havoc in their path. Eventually, the larvae become flies themselves, but the damage to your rabbit has been done.

Fly strike and maggots will be less likely to occur if your rabbit is kept indoors or in a screened hutch. Older, overweight, quiet rabbits will be more likely to get maggots. Rabbits with urine scald or skin problems at the perineum are also more likely to get maggots. Flies especially prefer the perineal region.

If your rabbit is afflicted with maggots, you may notice wet, irritated skin or matted hair, and, if you look closely, you should be able to find the maggots themselves. A rabbit with maggots should be taken to a veterinarian for treatment in which the maggots and all the dead tissue must be removed. The rabbit will also be given antibiotics and you will receive instructions on how to treat the wounds at home.

In some cases, there are so many maggots that the rabbit will become toxic. The maggots can also cause so much tissue damage that the rabbit may not survive.

Symptoms: Moving larvae, matted hair, moist hair, bleeding

Cause: Larvae laid by flies

Treatment: Remove maggots and dead tissue; antibiotics; wound care

Prevention: A screened hutch; healthy skin; prevent obesity

Malocclusion

A malocclusion is a misalignment of the teeth in which the front teeth at the top do not properly match those at the bottom. Malocclusion is a breeding issue, as adult rabbits with poorly aligned teeth will pass this trait on to their young.

Rabbits' teeth grow continuously at a rate of 3.9 to 4.7 inches (10 to 12 cm) a year. If the teeth are not worn down and do not press against each other, they will overgrow, leading to quite bizarre twists and turns of the teeth as they grow. Of course, this interferes with the rabbit's ability to eat properly.

You can tell if your rabbit has a malocclusion because the front teeth will not line up properly. The bottom incisors should sit just behind the top incisors so that they hit against the small peg teeth. The peg teeth are a small second set of incisors immediately behind the front incisors that you can see. Eventually, at least one set of incisors (usually the lower) will overgrow the other set. If this happens, you will need to trim your rabbit's teeth back to a normal position. If you do not have experience trimming teeth, you should let your veterinarian show you the technique. Some people take their rabbits to the veterinarian every four to six weeks to have the teeth trimmed; others learn how to do it themselves at home.

If you would like to do it yourself, be very patient. He is not likely to appreciate having metal instruments stuck in his mouth and you must be sure not to injure any of the delicate mouth tissues. Rescoe-type nail trimmers or wire cutters can be used to trim the teeth. A set of incisors should be trimmed together so that they will be the same height.

Trimming the teeth: Gently open the rabbit's mouth and hold the tongue away from the teeth. Some people use a tongue depressor or something similar to hold the tongue away from the teeth. Place the cutters around both teeth at the level to which the teeth should be cut back and cut, but watch out for flying pieces of teeth! Sometimes you may accidentally cut the teeth further than you wanted them to go. They will grow out. If the tooth is fractured below the gum line, however, antibiotics are sometimes recommended to prevent an infection from developing below the gum line. A tooth broken below the gum line does not always grow back.

Molars: In addition to the incisors, rabbits have molars in the back of their mouths that few people see. When veterinarians want to check on the molars, they usually use the same device that is used to look in people's ears, an otoscope. The molars can also overgrow. When they do, they develop sharp edges that cut into the inside of the cheeks, which can result in an excessive amount of drool being produced and running out of the mouth. This is also known as slobbers. If a lot of saliva falls to the dewlap or feet and sits there, it can cause irritation and infection.

Your veterinarian can trim the sharp edges of the molars or file them down. This usually requires anesthesia. If you think your rabbit has a tooth problem, do not wait to take him in to your veterinarian.

Symptoms: Overgrown teeth, teeth that do not line up properly

Cause: Heritable defect in the position of the teeth

Treatment: Trim teeth regularly to their normal position

Prevention: Do not breed rabbits with malocclusions

Mastitis

Mastitis is an inflammation or infection of the mammary glands, found on the rabbit's belly. Unless your doe is breeding, there is very little chance of her developing mastitis.

When a rabbit is about to deliver her litter, her mammary glands will begin to fill with milk to feed the kits. The ducts in the glands open up to deliver the milk, and, of course, as soon as the kits are born, they begin nursing.

Mastitis occurs as a result of bacteria moving up the duct and into the gland. Often, there is an abnormality of the gland, some trauma to the gland or nipple, or a poorly kept environment that results in the mastitis.

If the mastitis is not caught right away, the kits will receive infected milk and die. You should check your doe every day while she is nursing to see if her glands appear especially swollen or red. A severe case of mastitis will cause the mammary glands to turn a blue color. At this point, the doe is likely to show signs of illness as well. She may be depressed and running a fever. She may eat less and drink more.

Antibiotics dispensed by your veterinarian will be necessary to treat the mastitis. If only one gland is involved, you may be able to cover it so that the kits can still nurse from the healthy glands. Check with your veterinarian. In some severe cases, the mammary glands have had to be removed surgically.

Symptoms: Firm, hot, swollen mammary glands, red- or dark blue-colored mammary glands, depression, fever, anorexia, increased drinking

Cause: Poor sanitation, trauma to the mammary gland or teat

Treatment: Antibiotics; warm compresses; fluid therapy; surgery

Prevention: Good sanitation; nonabrasive environment

Milkweed Poisoning

Milkweed poisoning has been noted only in the southwestern United States. It occurs when rabbits are fed hay that contains the wooly pod milkweed, which has a resinoid that is toxic to rabbits. A rabbit needs to eat only 0.25 percent of his weight in green milkweed to die from it.

Affected rabbits develop paralysis of the neck muscles and lose coordination. As a result, it has also been referred to as "head down disease." If a rabbit has not eaten a fatal dose, he may survive as long as he is given a lot of nursing care to help him eat and drink while he is recovering.

Symptoms: Paralyzed neck, lack of coordination

Cause: Ingestion of wooly pod milkweed

Treatment: Supportive care

Prevention: Avoid milkweed-contaminated hay

Myiasis

Myiasis is a horrible name for an odd problem. It is also called warbles and is a disease of rabbits that are kept outdoors and exposed to flies. A larva from a *Cuterebra* fly invades the skin, usually at the neck or perineum. You will see a cone-shaped swelling with an open pore. The larva breathes through the pore. An affected rabbit may have more than one larva invading it.

Some rabbits will show no symptoms other than the swellings. Other rabbits can become quite ill with a long-term infection, and will become debilitated.

The larva needs to be removed because of the damage it causes, but it must be removed very carefully as crushing the larva can cause a fatal toxic shock to your rabbit. Veterinarians will often try to anesthetize the larva to remove it safely.

Symptoms: Swellings in the skin with an air pore

Cause: Cuterebra flies

Treatment: Removal of the larvae

Prevention: Screened housing for outdoor rabbits to prevent flies on them

Adult Checkered Giants weigh over 11 pounds.

Myxomatosis

Myxomatosis is also known as big head disease and is caused by a virus. It is usually transmitted through mosquitos, but can also be transmitted through ticks and fleas. An affected rabbit will first show swollen eyes. His temperature can reach as high as 108°F (42.2°C). The virus progresses through the face, causing the nose and ears to swell, and often killing the rabbit. If the rabbit survives, he will likely have the chronic form of the disease and his face will be covered in warts. Secondary bacterial infections are common when rabbits have this virus and can also lead to the death of the rabbit.

The myxomatosis virus has been released in Australia and New Zealand to help control the wild rabbit population there. Fortunately, this is not a disease that is commonly seen in the United States; however, there have been outbreaks in coastal areas of California and Oregon where the California brush rabbit acts as a reservoir for the virus. The cottontail and jackrabbit appear to be highly resistant to it. In European countries where the virus does exist, a vaccine is available to prevent infection.

Symptoms: Swollen eyes, swollen face

Cause: Myxomatosis virus

Treatment: Supportive care; antibiotics for secondary infections

Prevention: Good husbandry practices to minimize exposure to insect bites; vaccination (only in countries where myxomatosis commonly exists)

Orchitis/Epididymitis

This is a disease of male rabbits often caused by Pasteurella. When the Pasteurella bacteria is in the buck's testicles, it causes infection and swelling within the testicles (orchitis) or the connecting spermatic cords (epididymitis). Bucks will often have a fever as a result, eat less, and lose weight.

If your rabbit has this disease, he should be neutered. At the time your veterinarian removes both testicles, cultures should be taken. The cultures will often grow Pasteurella but may show Treponema instead. Treponema causes rabbit syphilis.

Symptoms: Swollen testicles or cords, lump on testicle, fever, anorexia, weight loss

Cause: Bacterial infection with Pasteurella or Treponema or bacteria from a wound

Treatment: Surgical removal of the testicles and cords

Prevention: Maintain Pasteurella-free stock; keep male rabbits apart

Papillomatosis

Papillomatosis is caused by one or more viruses. In one form of the disease, rarely seen in domestic rabbits in the United States, grayish warts are seen on the underside of the tongue or the floor of the mouth. The other form of the disease is known to occur in cottontail rabbits. It is caused by the Shope papilloma virus. Rabbits that have this virus will have horny warts on their necks, shoulders, ears, or abdomens. No serious consequences are associated with the infection and no treatment is given.

Symptoms: Warty growths in the mouth or on the body

Cause: Viral infection

Treatment: None

Prevention: Prevent exposure to infected rabbits

Pasteurella multocida

This is the bacteria most commonly associated with rabbits. Rabbits have a unique ability to harbor this damaging bacteria for long periods of time. Although carrier rabbits can go for extended periods without showing signs, ultimately there will be an outbreak of Pasteurella. The bacteria can be passed between a breeding pair and from a doe to her litter. She can pass it to her kits during delivery, by nursing, or from contaminated sipper tubes. Pasteurella can also be passed from rabbit to rabbit when one is actively infected.

When the Pasteurella bacteria does cause disease, it is usually in the respiratory tract—the nose and lungs—causing snuffles. Snuffles is a condition in which the rabbit's nose is congested, inflamed, and infected, causing a discharge from the nose and snuffling sounds. Snuffles occurs more frequently in the spring and summer. Often, you will see the nasal discharge on the front feet as the rabbit rubs his nose. Rabbits are also likely to have conjunctivitis, an inflammation of the tissues around the eyes, at the same time. Pasteurella is the number one cause of respiratory problems in rabbits. Respiratory problems are a major cause of disease and death in rabbits.

Pasteurella can also cause infections throughout the rabbit's body—in the middle ear, in the joints, or in any internal organ. These infections can often be treated with antibiotics and other supportive medications prescribed by your veterinarian, but your rabbit may still be carrying the Pasteurella bacteria. In breeding groups, rabbits carrying Pasteurella should be culled.

Symptoms: Nasal discharge, snuffling, runny eyes, head tilt or twisted neck, skin infection or ulceration, swelling under the skin, infertility

Cause: Pasteurella bacteria present in the rabbitry

Treatment: Antibiotics and supportive care for active infection

Prevention: Remove carrier rabbits from the group; purchase rabbits from Pasteurella-free stock; eliminate ammonia from the environment; maintain high husbandry standards; wean the young at four weeks if their mother is infected

Pododermatitis or Sore Hocks

The hock is the angular joint closest to the paw on a rabbit's hind leg. When a rabbit sits on poor flooring, the area below the hocks becomes chronically irritated and inflamed. That damage leads to secondary bacterial infections. This condition can also be caused by frequent thumping, obesity, or a small cage.

You will see that the hock area is reddened and may have discolored hair. You may also see some discharge from the skin. Early on, there are ulcerations, which progress to raised, thickened, scabbed lesions. This condition is very difficult to treat once it has settled in, so prevention is the best policy. If your rabbit is showing signs of sore hocks, change the hutch floor and bedding and take him to the veterinarian. After examining the rabbit, the veterinarian may wish to take radiographs to look for bone damage underneath the skin, and will likely start your rabbit on medication.

Symptoms: Ulcerated, reddened skin, stained hair, scabbing, infection

Cause: Poor flooring, obesity, frequent thumping, small cages

Treatment: Cleanse wounds; antibiotics

Prevention: Clean, nonirritating flooring; prevent obesity; supply adequate room

Posterior Paresis/Paralysis

Posterior refers to the back legs, paresis means that movement is limited by neurologic damage, paralysis means that use has been completely lost. In rabbits, the most common cause of paresis or paralysis is an injury to the lumbar portion of the back, the part of the back over the abdomen.

Back injuries in rabbits frequently result from poor handling that causes the rabbit to struggle or kick out.

Injuries can also occur if rabbits are startled or attacked in their cage. The vertebrae in the back can be fractured, or broken, from the trauma, or they can be moved out of place. In either case, the spinal cord is damaged at the same time. Because of the damage to the spinal cord, rabbits can lose bladder and bowel control as well as back leg movement.

If the spinal cord has been severed, there is no chance of the rabbit regaining use of his back legs. As a consequence, the rabbit's quality of life is extremely poor and most veterinarians will recommend euthanizing the rabbit. If the injury does not completely destroy the spinal cord, there is a limited opportunity for the rabbit to regain function of his legs.

Managing a paralyzed rabbit is a huge commitment and should not be undertaken lightly. These rabbits need nursing care throughout the day. They need protection from skin injuries and often need to have their bladder expressed throughout the day. It is reasonable to discuss euthanasia with your veterinarian if you have a paralyzed rabbit.

Symptoms: Loss of use of back legs

Cause: Injury to the back

Treatment: Surgery, medications, or no treatment depending on severity

Prevention: Always use proper handling techniques; keep predators away from the rabbit hutch

Pregnancy Toxemia

Pregnancy toxemia is caused by inadequate nutrition in pregnant does

or does that think they are pregnant (a false pregnancy or pseudopregnancy). It occurs late in pregnancy or after delivery. Dutch, Polish, and English breeds have a higher incidence of pregnancy toxemia than other breeds. Rabbits with toxemia become depressed and weak. They may become uncoordinated and even have convulsions. Rabbits can die of toxemia within hours. If you suspect this condition in your rabbit, she can be treated by a veterinarian with IV fluids and dextrose (sugar).

Symptoms: Weakness, lethargy, seizures

Cause: Inadequate nutrition during pregnancy

Treatment: IV fluids and dextrose

Prevention: High-energy diet for late pregnancy; avoid fasting; prevent obesity in does

Pyometra

This is primarily a disorder of breeding does. It can develop in does that have never been bred but have not been spayed. The lining of the uterus can become inflamed, which can sometimes happen after giving birth. The inflammation of the uterus is called metritis. If there is a bacterial infection in the uterus—often from Pasteurella or Staphylococcus—the condition is called pyometra. When this happens, the rabbit will often have a larger abdomen and will become weak and eat less. Frequently, there will be an abnormal discharge from the vagina.

Your veterinarian will confirm the diagnosis of pyometra. He or she can often feel the enlarged uterus. Radiographs or an ultrasound may be done to confirm the diagnosis.

Although you would expect antibiotics to be able to cure this infection, that is rarely the case. The best, most effective treatment is surgery to remove the inflamed or infected uterus.

Symptoms: Vaginal discharge, distended abdomen, anorexia, lethargy

Cause: Nonspecific

Treatment: Usually surgical removal of the uterus followed by antibiotic therapy

Prevention: Spay any does that will not be used for breeding

Red Urine

Red urine is not actually a disease, but it is a common concern of rabbit owners. It is natural to think that red-colored urine indicates that blood is present and something must be very wrong with your pet. Fortunately, that is not usually the case. Most cases of red-colored urine are due to the presence of a plant pigment called porphyrin. This is completely normal and is not a reason to be concerned. In most rabbits, the yellow color will return within a couple of days. It is possible that some rabbits eating the same food will have red urine and some will have the normal yellow urine. Interestingly, there are more cases of red urine in the fall and early winter.

If the urine does not return to its normal color, or if there are other signs that something is wrong, you should have your rabbit's urine evaluated. By testing the urine, your veterinarian will be able to tell you if blood is present. Signs that there is a problem include not eating, straining to urinate, urinating frequently, or urinating small amounts at a time. Conditions that can cause true blood in the urine include trauma, uterine cancer, polyps, kidney disease, and bladder disease.

Symptoms: Red-colored urine

Cause: Usually harmless plant pigments; in rare cases, blood in the urine

Treatment: None, unless there is blood present

Prevention: For actual blood in the urine: reduce the risk of trauma; spay and neuter rabbits

Respiratory Disease

The most common cause of disease in the nose, airways, and lungs is infection from the Pasteurella bacteria (previously described). Other bacteria and agents can also cause disease, such as the bacteria Bordetella bronchiseptica. Bordetella can cause damage to the respiratory tract of rabbits, dogs, cats, and guinea pigs. Dogs and cats can actually be vaccinated against this agent, which commonly causes kennel cough. If your pet has active kennel cough, it should be kept away from your other pets. When rabbits are infected with Bordetella, they have a discharge from the nose and can develop pneumonia. Once exposed, the infection is often complicated by other bacteria such as Pasteurella.

If your rabbit has a nasal discharge, snuffles, or is working harder to breathe, take him directly to your veterinarian. After identifying which bacteria, or combination of bacteria, are causing the problem, your veterinarian can choose an appropriate antibiotic to treat the infection. If your veterinarian determines that there is not a bacterial infection, allergies or heart disease could be considered a cause of the symptoms.

Symptoms: Nasal discharge, snuffles, faster or heavier breathing

Cause: Bacterial infection, allergies, heart disease

Treatment: Antibiotics for infection; corticosteroids and antihistamines for allergies; heart medications for heart disease

Prevention: Keep your rabbit away from other rabbits carrying Pasteurella or other pets carrying Bordetella

Ringworm/Dermatophytosis

Despite its name, ringworm is not actually a worm. It is a fungal disease that classically causes a round area of hair loss and redness. It is because of these round or ringlike areas that it is called ringworm. There are several types of fungi that can cause ringworm. Rabbits typically get a variety called Trichophyton.

A rabbit with ringworm will have areas of hair loss that are dry and crusty. He may also be itchy. The legs, feet, and head are most often

The black Holland Lop.

affected. There are treatments for ringworm but many cases will go away on their own. The challenge is to eliminate ringworm from the environment so that the rabbit does not get it again or pass it on. A dilute bleach solution can be used to clean any areas or equipment exposed to ringworm.

Ringworm is contagious among rabbits and to other animals as well. Humans can also be exposed and get very itchy, red, scaly lesions where they came in contact with the fungus.

Symptoms: Dry, crusty skin where hair is gone, itching

Cause: Fungus, usually Trichophyton

Treatment: None, or topical cream from veterinarian

Prevention: Keep rabbits away from any other animal carrying ringworm

Syphilis

Syphilis in rabbits is caused by *Treponema cuniculi.* It is not the same as syphilis in people and cannot be transmitted from rabbits to humans or vice versa. Syphilis is transmitted from rabbit to rabbit through venereal, or sexual, contact. The more times a rabbit is mated, the more likely it will get syphilis.

When rabbits develop syphilis, they become very sore, so they will not breed. Wounds will appear on the genitalia and the skin around the genitalia. First, the area appears red; later, the area will swell and form ulcers and scabs. In 15 percent of cases, lesions will be seen on the nose as well.

Symptoms: Sore vent, failure to breed

Cause: Treponema cuniculi transmitted by another infected rabbit

Treatment: Antibiotics for all exposed rabbits

Prevention: Infected individuals should not be permitted to breed

Tyzzer's Disease

Tyzzer's disease is caused by exposure to a bacteria, Clostridium piliforme. Stress from breeding or poor conditions will contribute to its development. Once a rabbit is infected, the rabbit will develop diarrhea, become depressed, and may die. This disease is a cause of severe diarrhea and death in rabbits 6 to 12 weeks of age.

Clostridium bacteria form spores that stay in the environment. In order to kill them, you can treat the environment with a 0.3 percent sodium hypochlorite solution, which is bleach heavily diluted with water.

Symptoms: Profuse diarrhea, depression

Cause: Clostridium piliforme bacteria

Treatment: Supportive care; fluids; high-fiber diet

Prevention: Good husbandry; low-stress environment

Urinary Incontinence

A rabbit with incontinence will drip urine, often without knowing that he is doing it, and have urine scald. Urine scald occurs when urine drips on the skin as it comes out. This is very irritating to the skin and discolors the hair.

Virtually all the time, incontinence is a result of an underlying medical problem. Rabbits with kidney or bladder problems including stones and high calcium in the urine will often have urine scald. Spayed rabbits sometimes develop a weaker bladder sphincter muscle and become incontinent, which can be helped by giving the rabbit replacement estrogen hormone.

Another common cause of incontinence is a neurologic problem because of damage to the spinal column. This can be anything from a back fracture to a protozoan infection in the spinal column. Your veterinarian is best qualified to investigate the cause of the incontinence. As soon as you recognize the problem, you should start cleaning and drying the perineum every day.

Symptoms: Dripping urine, urine scald

Cause: Kidney or bladder problems, weak bladder sphincter, back injury

Treatment: Specific for the cause

Prevention: Prevent back injuries; supply a proper diet

Urolithiasis

Urolithiasis is simply stones in the urinary tract, usually in the bladder. It is important before talking about stones to know that rabbits can normally have very large amounts of minerals in their urine. These minerals, mostly calcium, often form small crystals that show up on a radiograph. The heavy calcium in the urine can make the bladder show up more strongly than bone. Anyone looking at a radiograph of the abdomen must be very careful not to misinterpret these mineral crystals in the urine as stones.

Rabbits that are overweight, fed as many pellets as they want, and fed alfalfa hay are more likely to have a lot of calcium in their urine. Often, the urine of these rabbits will be cloudy and thick.

Because of the high level of calcium in the urine, the calcium often crystallizes, then the crystals may begin to stick together and form stones. Stones in the kidneys and bladder can form from other minerals as well.

Once a stone has formed, a rabbit may have difficulty urinating or have blood in the urine. Sometimes, you will notice a rabbit hunching his back or grinding his teeth from the discomfort. A urinary stone can also cause a rabbit to stop eating and become depressed.

Most stones can be identified by having a radiograph taken. If it is still not clear if the rabbit has a stone, an ultrasound should be done. Often, surgery is necessary to remove the stone(s).

The best way to prevent urinary stones from forming is to feed your rabbit properly so that he does not get too much calcium and does not become overweight. Also make absolutely certain that fresh water is available at all times. Talk to your veterinarian about any other factors that may specifically predispose your rabbit to form stones.

Symptoms: Difficulty urinating, blood in the urine, hunching the back, teeth grinding, decreased appetite, lethargy

Cause: No specific cause; factors include: high calcium level in the diet, obesity, structural abnormalities in rabbit's urinary system, limited exercise

Treatment: Usually surgery to remove the stones

Prevention: Proper diet with limited calcium intake; adequate exercise; weight control

Uterine Adenocarcinoma

This is an aggressive cancer of the uterus. The tumor grows slowly over 12 to 24 months and spreads throughout the body. Rabbits with this tumor often have vaginal bleeding that can be confused with blood in the urine. Affected rabbits also tend to become aggressive and often have cystic mammary glands.

As rabbits age, their incidence of uterine cancer increases dramatically. Does over four years old have a 50 percent chance of getting uterine adenocarcinoma and the risk increases every year. The only way to prevent it is to have your doe spayed at a young age. Surgery is curative if the cancer has not yet spread outside the uterus.

Symptoms: Vaginal bleeding, cystic mammary glands, aggression

Cause: Cancer of the uterus

Treatment: Surgical removal of the uterus if the cancer has not spread

Prevention: Spay does at four to six months of age

Viral Hemorrhagic Disease

This disease has not been reported in the United States but it has been recognized in rabbits in Europe and China. Rabbits in some areas of Mexico have also been diagnosed with hemorrhagic disease. A vaccine is available in other countries to prevent rabbits from developing viral hemorrhagic disease. The vaccine is not used in the United States because we do not yet have the disease here.

Rabbits younger than two months of age are resistant to the calicivirus thought to cause this disease. Older rabbits contract it from exposure to contaminated feces or from contact with food and water bottles that have the virus left on them from infected rabbits. A dilute bleach solution will kill any virus left on these objects. Affected rabbits are depressed, anorexic, and run a fever. Other symptoms include low body temperature, inability to stay upright, and bruises or nasal bleeding. Infected rabbits will die, but some may die from the virus before showing signs.

Symptoms: Fever, depression, anorexia, bloody nose

Cause: A virus, likely a calicivirus, transmitted from infected rabbits

Treatment: No effective treatment

Prevention: Eliminate any rabbits with calicivirus; use effective cleaning practices

Chapter Six

Rabbit Behavior

Jumping, thumping, racing, chasing—how entertaining rabbits can be. Snuggling, sleeping, grooming, nibbling—this rabbit is the one for me.

Rabbits in the Wild

We can learn a lot about our pet rabbits by discovering how wild rabbits act. Rabbits are naturally ground creatures that are most active in the evening and at dawn. Some rabbits are active all night. Your pet rabbit is likely to prefer this same schedule. They eat plants and are very good tunnelers. That's good to know when you want to entertain your rabbit.

Wild rabbits can live in very large warrens, or communities, of up to 150 rabbits. The rabbits in a warren look out for each other by watching for predators and warning the rest of the group when one is near. They also share in the search for food and the care of the young. Warrens will have more bucks than does. They mate in the spring, with bucks flagging their tails to attract females.

Because rabbits live in large warrens, our pet rabbits are also social. They generally like being with a group. Because they are normally most active at dawn and dusk, this is the best time to feed them and play with them. As rabbits are natural diggers and tunnelers, it is a good idea to give them a place to do this where they will not hurt anything. If you do not offer a place for this, your rabbit may pick its own place, somewhere you are not happy with.

The normal hierarchical male behavior in the warren also tells us a lot. It explains why it is not safe for us to put two intact (not neutered) males together. They will fight for dominance. Males are also more likely to mark territory, as they would in the wild, if they have not been neutered.

Digging

Because rabbits in the wild dig to form burrows, digging is an important natural behavior for them. Young rabbits will be especially prone to digging, but just because it is "normal" does not mean that you have to tolerate your rabbit digging up your carpet.

You should provide an alternative place for your rabbit to dig. A carpet box or a tunnel box can work. Whenever you catch your rabbit digging in a place you do not want him to be, give him a firm verbal reprimand and put him in the box. When he digs in the assigned box, you can give him a small food treat as a reward. This is one of those things that take constant monitoring and reinforcement in the beginning. If you do not catch your rabbit every time he is trying to dig up your carpet, you will not be able to give him consistent direction.

Vocalizations

Rabbits can be quite communicative at times; the trick is learning to understand what your rabbit is trying to tell you. Sometimes, your rabbit will tell you things by making sounds, using his voice; for example, he may growl when he is in an aggressive mood. Rabbits will also squeal or scream when something bad happens to them, or when caught or in pain.

A buck that wants to breed may purr. It is part of his way of telling a doe that he is interested. Rabbits may also gnash or grind their teeth, which can be a sign of pain. If you are not sure what your rabbit is trying to tell you with his voice, pay attention to what else is going on. Check his attitude and body position. This will help tell you what his voice is saying.

Body Talk

Thumping
Rabbits will pound a back leg against the floor or ground as a warning signal. This is called thumping. Rabbits may also thump by hopping with both back legs but staying in one place. Sometimes, they will also urinate.

Humans are most likely to see thumping when their pet rabbit is anxious or stressed. Some rabbits will thump when you are moving toward them or attempting to pick them up. This is a warning sign to you. If your rabbit is not yet used to being handled, or frightens easily, the thumping may be followed by an attack. Rabbits may thump to get what they want, such as more food. Or they may thump to try to keep you from herding them back into their cage.

Body, Ears, Tail Position
There are other ways a rabbit will use his body to communicate with you. If he is about to attack, his body will be stiffly upright and his tail will be stretched. He may also lay his ears toward the back of his head. On the other hand, if the rabbit is stiff with his ears back but is sitting, he is in a defensive position. A defensive rabbit is considering an attack.

You can learn a lot from your rabbit's body language.

Marking

If you have a male, you may notice him rubbing his chin around the house and around his cage. He is marking his territory. Rabbits have scent glands on the head, and the scent is rubbed onto things that the rabbit considers within his territory. Any other rabbits passing by would know that this territory belongs to another rabbit.

Wanting Attention

Some rabbits will be very clear with you about when they want attention and when they do not. If your rabbit nudges you with his muzzle, he wants attention. If he

scratches on the floor with his front paw, he may also be asking for attention. While you are petting your rabbit, he may nudge your hand away. He is clearly saying, "Thanks, but that is enough. Please stop." Your rabbit is also trying to tell you he does not want your attention if he struggles as you pick him up.

A rabbit may nip you to get your attention or to get you to do what he wants you to do. This nip is different from an aggressive bite. The appropriate response is to give out a loud shriek to let your rabbit know that he hurt you. Believe it or not, hurting you was not your rabbit's intention; getting your attention was. If you scream every time your rabbit nips you, your rabbit will learn to nip gently or not to do that at all.

Other Body Language

• When your rabbit licks or nuzzles you, it means that he likes you very much.

• If he is sitting up on his haunches in his cage, he wants to be let out.

• If he is out of his cage and sitting up, he is likely on the watch. This is how rabbits check for predators in the wild.

It is important to learn to "read" your rabbit so that you can build a good relationship with him. It is important that he learn to trust you. A good way to start is to not grab for him or hold him against his will. If your rabbit is not ready to have you pick him up, you can still give him attention and bond with him by rubbing around his ears or rubbing your chin against his face while he is on the floor.

Aggression

We like to think of rabbits as sweet, timid little animals. They may run but we do not expect them to fight. The truth is that all rabbits are capable of aggression under certain circumstances, such as intense fear. A very few rabbits will act aggressively without much provocation.

A mean rabbit can be very difficult, and even a little scary, at first. Rabbits can bite hard and kick hard. Their fast movements can make them difficult to work with during an aggressive moment. Have heart. Even if you have a rabbit that shows

some aggressive tendencies, he can eventually become the companion and family pet you want.

Disciplining the Rabbit

All animals, like children, need love, respect, and boundaries. This is doubly true for aggressive rabbits.

1. Your rabbit first needs to understand that you are not trying to hurt him. Take special care not to scare him.

2. Your rabbit also needs to understand that he does not have free rein. For starters, this should mean limiting his area to one room and not allowing him on the furniture.

3. Your rabbit should be trained not to chew and dig. Whenever you provide training for any behavior, it has effects on other behaviors. The training itself helps you establish a relationship with your rabbit.

Dominance

Pay attention to the exact situations that bring on the aggression. Some rabbits will perform behaviors that are dominance-related. This rabbit is trying to be top rabbit in your house and you need to let him know that you are "top rabbit." Some rabbits will try to show their dominance by urinating on your bed or favorite chair, or they will urinate in the cage of another rabbit to mark that territory as theirs and establish dominance. You can correct the behavior by denying your rabbit access to the spot he is going to. You can also make sure that your rabbit is supervised when he is out of his cage so that you can herd him away from the spot whenever he goes near it. A firm verbal reprimand when your rabbit approaches the spot may reinforce that area as off-limits. If that is not possible, you can set up an unwelcome surprise on the bed or chair for your rabbit by "booby trapping" the area with balloons or the safe mousetraplike devices you can get in pet stores to scare your rabbit off.

Nipping: Another way a rabbit may try to show dominance is by nipping you when you are sitting on a chair or couch. In this situation, your rabbit is trying to tell you that the place is rabbit territory and you had better leave. Your response is to tell your rabbit that the seat is your territory. Screech in response to the nip and gently, but firmly, place your rabbit on the floor, or gently press his head down, a means of establishing dominance. You will likely need to do this several times before your rabbit stops challenging you. If he does not seem to get what you are trying to teach him, herd him back to his cage for a time-out. You should respect the cage as the rabbit's territory. Whenever possible, convince him to come out when you want him out of the cage rather than reaching in to grab him inside the cage.

Seeking a Mate

Hormonally active rabbits may also show aggression. If a rabbit is seeking a mate and none is available, the rabbit may show signs of aggression. Most commonly, the rabbit circles your feet, mounts you (or an object), and bites you. Spaying or neutering your rabbit will alleviate this problem.

Keep in mind that aggressive rabbits take more time to adjust than other rabbits. Be patient. You may feel sometimes that you have not made a lot of progress with your training and bettering your relationship. You will. *Be consistent.*

Coprophagy

If you watch your rabbit early in the morning, you may see him in a contorted shape with his head all the way around until he reaches under his tail. By watching very closely, you may be able to see that your rabbit is eating his stool. This is a natural behavior and it is important that you always allow your rabbit to do this even if you find it offensive.

This action is called *coprophagy.* Once a day, in the early morning, rabbits produce a soft stool that is different from their stool the rest of the day. These softer stools are called cecotropes. By eating the cecotropes, your rabbit is gaining added nutrition. The bacteria in the rabbit's gut manufacture B vitamins and protein that come out in the cecotropes. A rabbit that has stopped eating cecotropes, perhaps due to illness, can become deficient in vitamin B and develop an undesirable change in the bacteria in the gut.

Chapter Seven
Breeding Rabbits

I must start this chapter with a word of caution: Breeding any animal is a very serious responsibility and should not be undertaken lightly. In an ideal world, only the healthiest animals that are the best representatives of their breed would reproduce. Some may ask, why not allow all animals to breed indiscriminately? The simple answer is that, for pet animals, there would not be enough homes for all the progeny, and constant reproduction would take a tremendous physical toll on the animals. The quality and length of their lives would be severely reduced. Even when animals are used for production reasons, such as being raised for their meat or fur, there must be limits. If animals bred indiscriminately, the quality of the animals would decrease over time. There would also be the same issues about quality and length of life.

So, now, I take a deep breath and strongly encourage any owner of a pet rabbit not to allow his or her pet to breed. The information given in this chapter should be used for

A Dwarf Rabbit peeks out from a flower patch.

interest's sake and/or if you are in the position of having brought home a female rabbit that is already pregnant. To prevent unplanned pregnancies, you should keep females separated from males until they are spayed and neutered. Some rabbit breeds are capable of reproducing at only four months of age. Although we still think they are babies, they do not.

Determining the Sex of Your Rabbit

Figuring out whether a rabbit is male or female can take some practice. It becomes easier to tell as the rabbit gets older. The only way to tell a male from a female rabbit is to check the sex organs. Don't worry. Your rabbit won't be embarrassed if you check.

At a few weeks to a few months of age, you will be able to tell a male from a female by looking at the rabbit's back end underneath the tail. It is easiest to look at this area with the rabbit on his or her back. Your index finger and thumb can be used to

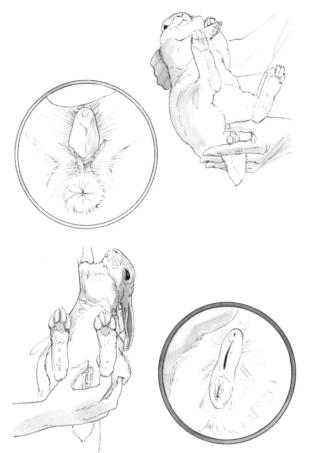

Identifying a male rabbit (above) and a female rabbit (below).

scrotal sacs located underneath his body and between his back legs. Sometimes, the testicles will slide in and out of the scrotum back inside the body. Both males and females have nipples, so do not use that as a determination.

If you have more than one rabbit and are not entirely sure about their sexes, have them checked by a veterinarian or an experienced rabbit breeder. Males may fight with each other; a male and female left together may breed at just a few months of age. You don't want these unexpected complications just because you were not sure.

Spaying and Neutering/Castrating

If your rabbit will be a pet, I strongly encourage you to spay your does and neuter your bucks. This can be done at four to six months of age, before sexual maturity. Rabbits that have been spayed and neutered live longer and are better pets. Males will be less likely to fight and neutering will eliminate urine spraying; for females, spaying will eliminate the risk of ovarian, uterine, and mammary cancers. Neutered pets also tend to be calmer and easier to train. They tend to be more affectionate and less destructive.

When performed by a skilled veterinary surgeon with rabbit experi-

gently push out the female vulva or male prepuce, the haired skin that covers the penis. In males that are a few months old, you may even be able to gently push out the penis itself from inside the prepuce.

The female's vulva is a V-shaped opening with a central slit. The male's prepuce is a small circle of raised skin with a very small hole in the middle. As a male rabbit gets older—over 12 weeks—you will be able to detect his testicles in the

ence, the risk of the surgery is very low. Rabbits should not be fasted prior to the surgery because there is no risk of them vomiting under anesthesia. Rabbits can eat and drink right up to the surgery and as soon after the surgery as they are interested in food. An overly full stomach can compromise the rabbit's breathing when he is laid on his back for the surgery, since the chest cavity is so small. At this time, the preferred anesthetic for rabbits is isoflurane gas. Some surgeons will also use a sedative or pain reliever.

A spay is an ovariohysterectomy. The ovaries and uterus of the female are removed through an incision in the midline of her abdomen, then sutures are placed inside and may or may not be placed in the skin. Some surgeons use surgical glue to close the skin so that the rabbit will not bite at sutures.

A neuter or castration is an orchiectomy. Males have their two testicles removed through incisions made directly over each testicle. Although two layers of sutures are placed inside, there may not be any sutures placed in the skin. Sometimes, surgical glue is used on the skin and you may see a blue color at the incision from it.

Note: Researchers have pioneered a vaccine that blocks pregnancy in rabbits. This single-dose vaccine has been proven to effectively prevent pregnancy for over six years. Even when the vaccine becomes available, however, it may not prove to be the best option for pet rabbits since the vaccine does not eliminate the hormones that lead to behavioral problems and uterine disease; only spaying and neutering a rabbit does. Keep your ears and eyes open for new developments.

Sexual Maturity

Different breeds of rabbits become sexually mature at different ages. Sexual maturity is the age at which all the right hormones are present and active and all the body parts work. This means that sexually mature animals are capable of making babies. In general, small breeds of rabbits are able to reproduce at a younger age than large-breed rabbits. For breeds that weigh 4 pounds (1.8 kg) and under, maturity occurs at four to five months of age. Medium breeds weighing 5 to 9 pounds (2.3–4.1 kg) will tend to reach sexual maturity at five to six months of age. Breeds weighing 10 to 12 pounds (4.5–5.5 kg) will likely mature by six or seven months of age, and even the largest breeds of rabbits, those weighing over 12 pounds (5.5 kg), will be able to reproduce at eight months or more. Bucks tend to be a little slower to mature than does and may not show much interest in does at an early age. You should first see the buck's testicles descend into the scrotal sacs at 12 weeks.

Breeding

Rabbits that are to be bred should be fed carefully to make sure that they are very healthy but not overweight. Fat rabbits will have trouble with breeding and delivery. Animals that are in poor condition should never be bred, as the added stress and demands of mating and breeding would be too much for them. It is important to keep females and males separated until it is time for a planned breeding.

The optimal age to breed does is starting before they are six months old and continuing until they are three to five years old. Larger breeds of rabbits are often not bred for the first time until they are slightly older. Some does will continue producing litters when they are even older than five. Rabbits that do not begin breeding at a young age rarely breed, which is why they are bred for the first time at such a young age. Bucks may mature about a month later than does.

Induced Ovulation

Rabbits are induced ovulators; they do not have heat cycles in the way that many other animals have. For many animals, the female is in heat and receptive to breeding and conception for a short period followed by a longer period when she cannot conceive. In general, does are receptive to breeding for 7 to 14 days, then not receptive for two. There will not necessarily be any warning signs that your female is receptive to breeding or is old enough to be bred. Some does will show signs that their hormones are active and they are receptive to breeding by rubbing their chins on their cage or by developing a swollen, purplish vulva. As an induced ovulator, the doe will release eggs from her ovary when she is mated. Eggs are released from the ovaries 10 to 13 hours after a breeding. This gives the best chance of the eggs being in the right place at the right time to meet the sperm.

Pseudopregnancy

In pseudopregnancy (false pregnancy), the doe seems to be pregnant or acts as if she is pregnant, but she actually is not. The false pregnancy usually lasts 15 to 17 days. This situation may occur if the doe is kept near bucks, if a buck mates with her but does not pass sperm, or if she is mounted by other does.

Breeding Methods

There are different methods for breeding rabbits, including artificial insemination. The most common is the natural method:

• The doe is taken to the buck's cage. The buck should not be taken to the doe's cage.

• The buck may chase the doe around for awhile, mate with her—usually within a couple of minutes—and then fall off her.

• After the doe and buck have mated once or twice, the doe should be returned to her own cage.

A healthy diet is crucial for rabbits if you intend to breed.

• Some breeders will allow the buck and doe to breed once and then bring the doe back 8 to 12 hours later for a second breeding to increase the chance of pregnancy and a larger litter. About 85 percent of breedings will result in litters as long as the rabbits are healthy.

Kindling

The gestation period, or length of pregnancy, is 28 to 32 days for rabbits; 90 percent of the growth of the kits in the uterus occurs in the last 10 days, the last trimester. The birthing process is called kindling.

Diet for the Doe

During the pregnancy, the doe must be fed a special high-quality diet to keep up with the demands of her body. During the last two days of her pregnancy, the doe should cut back on her food intake. If she does not, it should be limited for her to prevent diet-related medical problems such as ketosis or mastitis at delivery. The doe should eat only 50 percent of her normal diet two days before delivery, then the amount of food she receives should gradually increase after kindling. The amount should be increased every day after delivery until she reaches her full diet amount one week after delivery.

Nest-Kindling Box

Pregnant does should be provided with a nest-kindling box about 26 days into the gestation period. The box should be just a few inches larger than the doe, with clean straw or shredded paper used to fill it. The boxes can be purchased from pet supply houses or you can build one yourself out of plywood or particle board. The doe will pull some of her own fur from her dewlap, belly, and thighs to contribute to the nest.

The Birth

Kindling usually happens early in the morning. Although it often occurs very quickly, it can take as long as a day or two for the doe to deliver all the kits. The kits may come out head first or feet first. Fortunately, it is very rare for a rabbit to have a dystocia, a problem with delivery, so the doe should not need any assistance with the birth.

It is important that the doe not be disturbed during kindling. Excitement, stress, or noise can affect the delivery or cause the doe to injure her newborn kits. Although cannibalism is rare, it can occur if the doe is stressed. The kits should be checked only after the doe is recovered and relaxed from delivery. If a kit falls out of the nest, you must put him back in. Do not expect the doe to do this. She is not likely to stay with the kits at all times, nor should she be forced to.

The Kits

The average litter size for a medium-sized rabbit is seven to eight kits. Litter sizes range from only one kit to as many as 22! Kits are born hairless, blind, and deaf. Because rabbits have eight to ten mammary glands that produce milk, there is plenty of room for the average-sized litter to eat.

Kits should appear vital and have a full stomach, not a sunken stomach. If they have a full stomach, they are being properly mothered. When the kits are about ten days old and opening their eyes, they should be checked to make sure none of the eyes is stuck shut or infected.

Remember: The doe will need extra fresh, clean water while she is nursing.

In breeding programs, several does are often bred at the same time. Does will accept kits from another doe. If one rabbit has a large litter and another has a small litter, the number of kits can be spread around so they are all given their best chance to grow big and strong. If a doe is not giving her kits proper attention, they can also be transferred to a more attentive mother. When does are poor mothers, it is either because they were frightened at the time of kindling or they were poorly bred and have a nervous nature.

Weaning

Kits generally begin eating solid food after their eyes are open. They will continue to nurse milk from the doe until they are four to six weeks old. At this time, the doe will slow her milk production and the kits should be fully weaned onto solid food. The kits are usually kept together for another week or two before they are moved or separated.

Future Pregnancies

Do not be fooled into thinking that does cannot or will not be bred for awhile after they kindle; in fact, does may be receptive to breeding just 72 hours after kindling. Breeders should wait several weeks after kindling before breeding the doe again. One schedule is to breed the doe eight weeks after kindling, which will result in four litters born each year. To achieve five litters a year, a doe must be bred 42 days after kindling. Although more litters could be produced every year, it would take a tremendous toll on the doe and decrease her life expectancy and likely her health.

Newborns and Orphans

Your dog arrives at the backyard with a live young rabbit in his mouth, or you are mowing the yard and uncover a rabbit's nest complete with newborn or young rabbits. Has either of these scenarios ever happened to you? They are two of the most common reasons veterinarians and wildlife rehabilitators get questions on raising newborn rabbits.

Rabbits' Nests in the Wild

Let us first talk a little about rabbits in the wild and their nests. Nests are often in open areas such as lawns, but can also be found in tall grass or brush piles. The biggest surprise is that does spend very little time nursing their baby rabbits. Baby rabbits generally eat only once a day, in the early hours of the day while it is still night. When the mother is not nursing the babies, she is usually away from the nest; if she stayed in the nest, she would attract predators. So, the quiet, well-fed babies are left alone in a covered nest most of the time.

All of this is important to remember if you find a nest. You should never assume that the baby rabbits are abandoned simply because their mom is nowhere to be found. Unless you set up a 24-hour surveillance camera, you are not likely to catch her at the nest. If you are really concerned that the babies are not being cared for, you can check on them each morning and see if they are quiet, warm, and round-bellied. If they are, their mom is doing her job.

The bottom line here is this: If you find a nest, do your best to cover it over and leave the rabbits alone. The survival rate in the wild, even despite

Baby rabbits are cute, but they grow very quickly.

predators and the occasional inattentive new mother, is much greater than the survival rate when hand-raised, which is less than 10 percent. Disturbing a nest will not mean that the mother will not come back to it. If you have disrupted the protective covering of the nest, you should find some way to replace it, such as with grass.

Normal Rabbit Development

Little rabbits grow very quickly and it is not long before they do not need their mother or us. Interestingly enough, contact with siblings is much more important than contact with the doe except for feeding. If newborn rabbits do not have contact with their siblings, they will gain less weight, have more trouble reproducing later on, and be less active.

Wild cottontails develop a full coat of fur within one week. At six to ten days, they will open their eyes. At three weeks, they are weaned and no longer taking their mother's milk. Although they are eating on their own at three weeks, rabbits will continue to return to the nest to sleep after their explorations for a few more weeks. So, if you see a very small rabbit hopping around your yard, let him go on his way. He is not lost or seeking help.

Pets and Wild Rabbits

What should you do if a pet brings a rabbit home? If it is a live rabbit, try to find the nest and put the rabbit back in it. Human or pet handling should not keep an attentive mother away from her babies. If you are having trouble finding the nest, watch your pet to find the location of the nest. Pets are likely to explore the same spot again. Remember that rabbits only eat once or twice a day. As long as you keep the baby warm and out of trouble, you should have a few hours to locate the nest and return the rabbit.

Once you know a nest exists, you must make sure your pets do not disturb it. That may mean leash-walking your dogs or keeping your cats inside for a period of time. You can also try to put an obstacle around the nest so that the doe can get in but a dog cannot.

Constructing New Nests

If a nest has been completely destroyed, you can construct a new one in a nearby location. The doe will go to the original spot and should then search nearby for her young ones. If they are crying, they will be easy for her to find. To make a new nest, dig a hole just a few inches deep and move as much material from the old nest to the new one as possible. Place the baby rabbits inside and use as much dry grass as you need to fill the nest and keep the babies warm. Cover the top of the nest with longer plant material. To test if the doe has

returned, you can lay a few twigs across the top of the nest and see if they have been disturbed the next day.

Hand-raising

If a young rabbit has been truly abandoned or if you cannot find the nest, the rabbit needs to be hand-raised. Only rabbits three weeks of age or younger should need raising, since wild rabbits are weaned by this time and have begun foraging for themselves. To help decide if the rabbit needs your assistance, look for these troubling signs:

- cold body
- thin body
- dehydration—seen as "tenting" of the skin when it is picked up, or brown urine
- constant crying
- sluggish movements
- sunken belly

These are all signs that the rabbit is in trouble. Before trying to raise a rabbit at home, contact a wildlife rehabilitator in your area. The rehabilitator will have a lot more knowledge and skill in raising orphaned wild animals than you have. You can locate a rehabilitator by calling your veterinarian, the animal control officer for your town, or your police department for a reference. It is especially important to get the rabbit to a wildlife rehabilitator or to a veterinarian who treats wild animals if the rabbit has been injured. Even a tooth wound from your pet is a life-threatening injury to a young rabbit.

Caring for an Orphaned Rabbit

Diet: The highest death rate among newborn rabbits is from hand-raising; therefore, wild rabbits are best left in or near their nest. A sick rabbit should be in the care of a wildlife rehabilitator or veterinarian. If those options do not exist, please follow the following diet recommendations—this is the same diet that should be used if your own rabbit refuses to care properly for her young:

• Get Esbilac puppy milk replacer made by Pet Ag at your veterinarian's office or a pet store. You can get the liquid or powder version. The liquid version is easier to use but the powder will last longer.

• Mix ⅓ cup Esbilac with ½ cup water. Feed a rabbit that is less than a week old 2 ml of this mixture twice a day with an eyedropper or a syringe (2 ml is just under ½ teaspoon; 5 ml is a teaspoon).

• If the rabbit will not eat his full meal, wait four to six hours and try to feed him the balance. The amount you feed can be doubled when the rabbit is a week old, and doubled again when he is two weeks old.

Rabbits should grow every single day at this age. If you are not sure if a rabbit is growing, you can use a postage scale to weigh him every day before you feed. Although you might think that more food is better, it is not—you can kill a baby rabbit simply by overfeeding it.

Some people use KMR, kitten milk replacer, also by Pet Ag, instead of Esbilac. KMR has been used without diluting it with water and without additives. KMR has been recommended at 2.5 ml given twice daily for the first week of life. When the rabbit is one week old, the amount is increased to 5–7.5 ml at each feeding. Two-week-old rabbits can handle 15 ml, or one tablespoon of KMR at each feeding. I do not have any personal experience with KMR in rabbits and nutritional data indicate that Esbilac is closer to rabbit milk than KMR is.

Organisms: One of the reasons the death rate is so high in hand-raised rabbits is that they start with a sterile gastrointestinal tract and when we feed them, we put in the wrong bacteria, not the ones they need. To counteract this, you can try to feed them the right organisms, which come only from other rabbits. If you have an older rabbit, try to collect the cecotropes—the soft droppings the rabbit usually eats. If you are able to collect a cecotrope, you can mix it with the milk and feed it to the infant rabbit. Add one cecotrope per day, for four to five days, in rabbits under a week of age.

Eliminations: After every feeding, you must stimulate the baby rabbit to urinate and defecate. You can do this by gently rubbing his backside under his tail with a damp nonabrasive cloth. Cotton or a soft washcloth can be used.

Offering other food: When the baby rabbit is ten days old, you can begin to offer him other foods such as very small amounts of alfalfa hay, dandelion greens, and vegetables. Rabbits should be completely weaned off milk by about three weeks of age.

Handling: While under your care, a wild baby rabbit should be handled as little as possible. This would be closest to his life in the rabbit nest. Excessive human handling is very stressful for him. Make a nest for the baby in your house by lining a small box with paper or a towel and fresh dry grass. Provide a small hiding place for him to use. Do not provide extra heat or leave the box in an overly warm place; room temperature of about 65 to 70°F (18.3–21.1°C) is comfortable for a baby rabbit. The nest should not need to be cleaned until the rabbit is eating on his own since he will be urinating and defecating only when you stimulate him after feeding during the first few days.

Releasing the infant rabbit: When a wild infant rabbit is eating on his own and moving quickly, it is time to release him into the backyard or another safe area. Do *not* keep a wild rabbit as a pet. Wild rabbits belong outside.

Understand that wild baby rabbits are likely to die under human care—the survival rate with hand-raising is 10 percent or less.

Genetics

Breeders use their knowledge of genetics to amplify the best characteristics of their rabbits and minimize or eliminate the undesirable heritable qualities.

Let's start with the basics. Genetics refers to the DNA blueprints that determine characteristics. In the rabbit, the genetic material is made up of 22 pairs of chromosomes. Each chromosome contains genes with the DNA that will determine how big the rabbit will be, what color his coat will be, and how his body is put together. Even attitude and ability to breed are partly determined by a rabbit's DNA. The DNA consists of two strands giving two copies of every gene. The doe and the buck each pass a copy of half of their DNA and genes onto their offspring; thus, the offspring will have characteristics of both parents. If the doe and buck are properly matched, the offspring will get the very best characteristics of each without any of the parents' less desirable characteristics.

Many, but not all, genes have a dominant form and a recessive form. That means that the very same place on two strands of DNA can give different instructions. If both genes are dominant, the rabbit will express the dominant trait; if the gene on both strands is the recessive form of the gene, the rabbit will express the recessive trait; if one gene is dominant and the other is recessive, the rabbit will show either the dominant trait or a third variation of the trait.

Color Genes

To give you an idea of how complicated DNA can be, there are ten genes that control the basic color of

Rabbits come in a variety of colors, as seen in this diverse group.

a rabbit's coat alone. These genes are called A, B, C, D, E, En, Du, Si, V, and W (a, b, c, etc. when recessive). In addition to these ten basic genes, other genes modify the color. These modifiers are not single genes. Multiple genes work together to modify the basic color. These modifiers are characterized as rufus modifiers, color intensifiers, and plus/minus (blanket/spot) modifiers. All together, you can get a tremendous number of combinations of these genes and their modifiers, which is what gives us the wonderful array of rabbit colors that we see.

As an example, if a rabbit has one dominant form of the En color gene and one recessive form, the rabbit will have spots. If the rabbit has two dominant En color genes, the rabbit will have spots only on its head, and if the rabbit has two recessive en genes, it will not have any spots at all. Other color patterns are caused by a complicated mix of genes. In order to have a lilac point-colored rabbit, the rabbit must have two recessive a genes, two recessive b genes, a recessive c gene specifically for the light chinchilla color, two recessive d genes, two recessive e genes, a dominant W gene and color-modifier genes. If even one of those genes is different, you cannot get a rabbit that is a lilac point.

Another example that shows the effect of dominant and recessive genes is the color of the Marten rabbit. The Marten breed has two colors:

the standard marten color and the dark marten color. Although it is not a breed color, albinos also factor into the coloration. An albino has two recessive color genes. The dark marten color is the dominant color gene and the dark marten color will occur only if two dominant genes are present. These marten colors show the classic simple heritable pattern of dominant-recessive traits. Breeding two albinos together will result in an all-albino litter. Breeding an albino rabbit with a dark marten-colored rabbit will result in all the progeny being standard marten in color. The standard marten-colored rabbits will have one recessive gene and one dominant. Remember, they will pass on only the recessive or the dominant gene when they mate. As a result, if you breed two rabbits with the standard marten color together, 25 percent of the progeny will receive only recessive genes and will be albino; 25 percent will receive two dominant genes and have the dark marten color. The other 50 percent of the progeny will receive one dominant gene and one recessive gene and have the standard marten color. This does not necessarily mean that if the rabbits have four kits, one will be albino, one will be dark, and the other two will be standard. These percentages are averages that will be proven over time.

Believe it or not, rabbit fur contains only two pigments, dark brown and yellow. If a rabbit's fur has no pigment at all, it will appear white.

The tremendous amount of color variation throughout the rabbit kingdom is based on different mixes and intensities of the dark brown and yellow pigments. Some rabbits' fur is so complex that individual hairs will have different amounts of pigment expressed along that single hair. Two hairs sitting right next to each other can even contain different amounts of the pigments.

As a general rule, longer-haired rabbits will have more dilute colors than shorthaired rabbits. Roughly the same amount of pigment is present in a shorthair and a longhair. Therefore, in a longhair, the pigment is more spread out and not as intense as the shorthair.

To sum up:
• All those many genes define how much dark brown and yellow pigment will be in the hair.
• They define whether there will be a lot of pigment or just a little.
• They set up whether the colors will be solid on the hair or blended in stripes through the hair.
• They even define when the hair will not have any color at all.

As complicated as the genetics of hair color may seem, it is but one small part of the genetic makeup of a rabbit. It would take many lifetimes of study to define all the genetic patterns of a rabbit. Good breeders will take the information that is available to make sure they breed the best-quality, healthiest rabbits. Fortunately, we get to enjoy them without all that hard work.

Chapter Eight
Showing Rabbits

Of course you've heard of dog shows and horse shows; well, there are also rabbit shows. These shows are a very popular part of the rabbit industry, where breeders compete against each other to show off their best rabbits. Raising show rabbits is a hobby that requires quite a commitment, since it takes a lot of time to raise good-quality rabbits. Breeders must be very selective in the breeding rabbits they choose, to be sure they advance and improve their breed. When you have a good-quality rabbit that wins a blue ribbon at a show, it is a thrilling experience.

The ARBA Standards

In the United States, standards for rabbits are established by the ARBA—American Rabbit Breeders Association, Inc. The Standard of Perfection describes in detail what each breed of rabbit should be. It covers everything from the proper size of the rabbit to his color and the density of his hair coat. Judges use the Standard of Perfection to evalu-

ate the rabbits entered in a show. The winning rabbit will be the one that most closely meets the standard. The judges also use guidelines for how to weigh different parts of the rabbit's look. For example, the quality of an Angora's wool counts 55 percent in its evaluation. The fur counts for only 8 percent of the score of the English Spot, but its markings count for 44 percent of its score. With other breeds, such as the Jersey Wooly, the dominant score comes from the body shape and size.

Forty-five breeds of rabbits are recognized by the ARBA and compete in rabbit shows. Some breeds win Best in Show a lot more often than others. In 1997 and 1998 the Mini Rex and the Satin breeds each had about 200 Best in Show wins. The American Fuzzy Lop, by comparison, won Best in Show only about 20 times each of those years.

ARBA Registration

The ARBA is the largest organization of its kind in the world. It also registers purebred rabbits that are

A typical rabbit show.

eligible for show. In order to register your rabbit for show, you must be a member of the ARBA and your rabbit must also have a three-generation pedigree, a family tree for your rabbit. It includes the name, breed, sex (male or female), variety, and date of birth of the parents, grandparents, and great-grandparents. The other requirements for registration with the ARBA are that the rabbit must be at least six months old, weigh what an adult of its breed should weigh, and be proven free of any disqualifying characteristic based on examination by a licensed registrar.

The ARBA takes further steps to identify registered animals. It has established a merit system to show how many prior generations have also met the standard for the breed.

• If a registered rabbit does not have registered parents, the rabbit will get a stamp on his certificate.
• If both parents are registered, the rabbit's certificate will carry a red seal.
• If both parents and all four grandparents are registered, the certificate carries a red and white seal.
• If all rabbits in all three generations are registered, the certificate will carry a red, white, and blue seal.

The certificate helps tell you whether your rabbit's relatives have been shown to meet the breed standard.

With the ARBA system, rabbits can be registered even if their parents are not, as long as they meet the requirements. The ARBA system also ensures that a rabbit is not registered based simply on his parents' qualifications. Each rabbit must be individually proven to meet the breed standard to become registered.

The Shows

The American Rabbit Breeders Association keeps track of upcoming shows and gives information about the shows through *Domestic Rabbits* magazine. The ARBA sanctions over 2,000 shows per year throughout the United States, Canada, and other countries. Some of these are small local shows with fewer than 100 entries. The largest rabbit show is the ARBA National Convention, where as many as 20,000 rabbits and cavies (guinea pigs) are entered.

If you are interested in entering your rabbit in a show, you fill out an official entry form and return it to the secretary for the show. You will be given a show catalog that contains all the instructions for the show. Make sure your rabbit is in his best condition and coat and then make sure you get him to the judging table at the right time.

Competition

Breeders take their finest rabbits to shows where the rabbits compete based on their appearance and how well they match the standard for their breed. Angora rabbits compete against other Angoras; Mini Lops compete against other Mini Lops. An experienced judge decides which of the rabbits at the show is the best representative of his breed and awards him a ribbon. The best of all the different breeds then compete against each other for the Best in Show award.

Points

Rabbits are awarded points based on the position in which they finish. A first place finish within the breed is awarded six points, a second place finish receives four points, third place receives three, fourth place receives two, and fifth place receives one point. These points are then multiplied by the number of rabbits shown in the class—the number of competitors. In that way, more points are awarded to a rabbit that wins over a greater number of competitors. A good breeder will want to breed a rabbit more heavily that has been shown to be a good representative of his or her breed.

Grand Champions

When a rabbit wins an award at a show sanctioned by the ARBA, he receives a Leg of Grand Champion. After three Legs are won, the owner can apply for a Grand Champion Certificate for that rabbit. Other requirements for Grand Championship include that the Legs be awarded under at least two different judges.

Cheating

There is such a thing as cheating for a show; if you cheat, your rabbit

This beautiful Florida White is worthy of a blue ribbon!

will be disqualified. Cheating would include such things as changing the color of the toenails so that they are the proper breed color or using silicone or polish on a coat to change its natural appearance.

Attending Shows

One of the best ways to prepare for shows is to attend one in which you do not have a rabbit entered. Watch carefully to see how the rabbits are kept and what the handlers—the people showing the rabbits—do to prepare. Watch the flow of events at the show, and observe how handlers position their rabbits on the table. It is okay to ask questions of the people running the show and of those who are showing as long as you choose your time properly. Do not ask questions when people are readying their rabbits for competition or are tied up in another task.

Chapter Nine

Rabbit Breeds

Just as with dogs, horses, and other animals, there are many different breeds of rabbits. Each breed has unique features that identify it as different from all other breeds. Interestingly, the breeds commonly seen in the United States are not always the same breeds you would find in other parts of the world. Standards for breeds commonly bred and shown in the United States are set by judges and breeders and approved by the American Rabbit Breeders Association, the ARBA.

Colors

Trying to identify all the color patterns rabbits can have is even more difficult than trying to keep track of all the breeds. Use this list for reference when you are looking at the colors that each breed can come in or when you are trying to decide what color your own rabbit is. If you would like more definition about the details of the color patterns, you might refer to the standards published by the American Rabbit Breeders Association.

Agouti: Bands of colors and ticking on each hair; this group includes chestnut, chinchilla, lynx, opal and squirrel

Black: Rich jet black; may have undercolor

Black Otter: Black body with a white or pale cream underside; the hair is orange at the junction of the two main colors

Blue: Rich, clear medium shade of blue or slate blue

Blue Otter: Blue color with fawn areas and fawn-tipped guard hairs

Blue Steel (Ticked): Overall blue color ticked with tan or silver

Blue Tortoiseshell: Blue and beige

Broken: White with any recognized breed color in a patched, spotted or blanket pattern; nose marking, eye circles, and colored ears are present

Brown Gray Agouti: Slate blue hair base followed by a medium tan band, a charcoal brown thin band, and a top band of lighter tan

Californian: Pure white body marked with black on the nose, ears, feet, and tail

Castor: Rich, dark brown top color over an intermediate ring of orange or red over slate blue under-color; light black tipping of hairs

Chestnut Agouti: Rich, brown shade with black ticking over an orange band and tan or slate undercolor

Chinchilla: A blend of pearl and medium slate or black ticked with black-tipped guard hairs

Chinchilla Agouti: Alternating bands of pearl and medium slate with black-tipped guard hairs

Cinnamon: Rust or cinnamon color

Chocolate: Rich, dark chocolate brown

Chocolate Agouti: Rich chestnut color on top of bands of tan, alternating with light chocolate

Chocolate Chinchilla: Blend of chocolate and pearl ticked with chocolate-tipped guard hairs

Chocolate Steel: Overall chocolate ticked with tan or silver (Ticked)

Chocolate Tortoiseshell: Creamy chocolate color and fawn color

Copper Agouti: Red color on top, lower bands of red-orange and dark slate; ticked with jet black-tipped guard hairs

Cream: Pinkish beige to almond color

Fawn: Rich, golden straw color

Frosted Pearl: Light pearl coat shaded with black, blue, chocolate, or lilac

Gray: Dark, uniform color consisting of three distinctly colored hairs: solid black, black with a narrow tan tip, and black with a narrow tan band near the tip; dark slate under-

color. This color is unique to the English Spot.

Light Gray: Agouti coat with slate blue color next to the skin; an intermediate band of off-white and a surface color of uniform light gray with black-tipped guard hairs

Lilac: Pinkish shade of pale gray

Lilac Chinchilla: Blend of lilac and pearl ticked with lilac-tipped guard hairs

Lilac Steel (Ticked): Overall lilac color ticked with tan or silver

Lilac Tortoiseshell: Lilac and beige

Lynx Agouti: Orange-silver color on top, bright orange middle, white undercolor; silver-tipped fur or a surface color of tan atop tan and light lilac bands with lilac-tipped guard hairs

Opal Agouti: Rich blue outer color, gold middle color, slate blue undercolor

Orange: Light orange to a bright orange

Pearl: Light pearl gray

Pearl (Shaded): Pearl or light body color shading to sable, black, blue, chocolate, or lilac on the nose, ears, feet, and tail

Pointed White: Pure white body with black, blue, chocolate, or lilac colored nose, ears, feet, and tail (Himalayan marked)

Red: Deep brown-red

Sable: Dark, rich sepia brown

Sable Marten: Siamese sable coloring with silver-white markings and silver-tipped guard hairs

Sable Point: Cream-colored body with rich sepia brown color on the nose, ears, feet, and tail

Sandy: Reddish sand color

Seal: Sable color, so dark that it is almost black

Self: Same color over the entire rabbit. This group includes black, blue, chocolate, lilac, blue-eyed white, and ruby-eyed white.

Shaded: Gradual transition of a color from dark to light. This group includes frosted pearl, sable, sable point, siamese sable, seal, tortoise, and siamese smoke pearl.

Siamese Sable: Rich sepia brown color on the ears, face, back, outside of legs, and upper side of tail, with a paler sepia color on the other body areas

Siamese Smoke Pearl: Smoke gray color on the ears, face, back, outside of legs, and upper side of tail, with a pearl gray-beige color on the rest of the body

Silver/Silver Fox: Silver over the entire body with white or white-tipped hairs

Silver Marten: Black, blue, chocolate, or lilac base color with silver-white markings and silver-tipped guard hairs

Smoke Pearl: Medium smoky blue shading to a light pearl gray-beige; other body areas dark smoky blue

Smoke Pearl Marten: Smoke pearl color primarily with silver-white markings and silver-tipped guard hairs

Squirrel: Alternating blue and pearl with blue-tipped guard hairs

Steel (Ticked): Dark charcoal or steel gray ticked with tan or silver

Tan Pattern: Markings (not necessarily tan in color) present in the fol-lowing areas: nostril, eye circles, jowls, insides of ear, belly, insides of leg, underside of tail. This group includes black otter, blue otter, sable marten, silver marten (black, blue, chocolate, lilac), smoke pearl marten, and tans (black, blue, chocolate, lilac).

Ticked: Solid or tipped guard hairs throughout the coat that are a different color than the body. This group includes silver/silver fox and steel.

Tortoise: Bright orange shaded with black, blue, chocolate, or lilac

Tortoiseshell: Orange and black or dark fawn and black

Tri-Colored: White in conjunction with any of the following sets of colors: dense black and golden orange, lavender blue and golden fawn, dark chocolate and golden orange, dove gray and golden fawn

White: Exactly what it should be: white

Wide Band: Basic color over the body, head, ears, tail, and feet; lighter color on eye circles, inside of ears, bottom of tail, jowls, and belly. This group includes cream, fawn, orange, and red.

Other terms that will help you wade through the descriptions:

Term and Definition

Band: An unbroken circle of marking color

Bar: A semicircle of marking color

Flyback: Condition that exists when the hair is pushed forward in an unnatural direction; it may or may not "fly back" into its original, natural position

List of Breeds

There are 45 breeds of rabbits recognized by the ARBA and many more that are well known in Europe. This chapter highlights specific features of the breeds, starting with a summary of the breeds recognized by the ARBA.

Small Breeds (2–6 pounds, 0.9–2.7 kg)

American Fuzzy Lop
Britannia Petite
Dutch
Dwarf Hotot
Florida White
Havana
Himalayan
Holland Lop
Jersey Wooly

Mini Lop
Mini Rex
Netherland Dwarf
Polish
Silver
Tan

Medium Breeds (6–9 pounds, 2.7–4.1 kg)

American Sable
Belgian Hare
English Angora
English Spot
French Angora
Harlequin

Lilac
Rex
Rhinelander
Satin Angora
Silver Marten
Standard Chinchilla

Large Breeds (9–11 pounds, 4.1–5 kg)

American
American Chinchilla
Beveren
Californian
Champagne d'Argent
Cinnamon
Crème d'Argent

English Lop
Giant Angora
Hotot
New Zealand
Palomino
Satin
Silver Fox

Giant Breeds (11 pounds, 5 kg, and over)

Checkered Giant
Flemish Giant
French Lop
Giant Chinchilla

Guard Hair: Stiff, longer hairs interspersed through the coat

Spine Marking: Strip of color starting behind the ear base and extending unbroken along the back to the tip of the tail

The Breeds

Alaska

Size: 6–8½ pounds (2.7–3.9 kg)
Color: Black

Despite its name, the Alaska breed comes not from Alaska but from Germany. It is not a breed recognized by the ARBA (American Rabbit Breeders Association). This is a twentieth-century rabbit bred so that its coat would resemble an Alaskan fox. The Alaska is a breed of rabbit that was produced in different places at different times. This happens more often than you might expect. Throughout history, devoted rabbit breeders have interbred different rabbit breeds to improve a breed or attempt to create a new one. As a result of these trials, breeders in different areas may produce rabbits with new but similar characteristics. The first time the breed was seen is thought to have been Germany in the 1920s as a result of crossings between Himalayan and Argentes rabbits. The breed arose separately in France by the 1930s. Finally, an identical breed was developed in England but became extinct by the 1930s. Its appearance is similar to that of the Havana.

American

Size: 9–12 pounds (4.1–5.5 kg)
Color: Blue, white

The American is a medium-boned rabbit with a broad body. Its body should be mandolin-shaped with an arch from the shoulders to the hips. The head is relatively narrow with erect ears. The ears should taper slightly at the end and be in proportion to the rest of the body. Does may have a small dewlap.

American Checkered Giant

Size: 11 pounds (5 kg) and more
Color: White with black or blue markings

This breed first came from Germany, not America. It is not a breed that is recognized by the ARBA. The Giant carries its body well off the ground and can be identified by a series of markings. The black or blue markings are seen as body spots, a butterfly pattern on the nose, eye circles, cheek spots, colored ears, and a spine marking.

American Chinchilla

Size: 9–12 pounds (4.1–5.5 kg)
Color: Chinchilla

The fur and its color are important considerations in the American Chinchilla. The ideal length of the fur is 1¼ inches (3.2 cm). The fur should be very dense and of a fine texture so that it is smooth and glossy. This is a well-rounded rabbit with a well-filled face and jaw. The erect ears are carried close together and are the same color as the body. The large, alert eyes are circled with a narrow strip of light pearl. The top of the tail is black; its underside is white.

American Fuzzy Lop

Size: 3½–4 pounds (1.6–1.8 kg)

Color: Chestnut agouti, lynx agouti, opal agouti, squirrel agouti, broken, black, blue, blue-eyed white, chocolate, lilac, ruby-eyed white, sable point, siamese sable, siamese smoke pearl, tortoiseshell, fawn, orange

The American Fuzzy Lop should be compact, balanced, and heavily muscled. It is a short rabbit with well-developed shoulders and hindquarters. The head should appear massive in relation to the body, and be broad. The head is held high and close to the shoulders. The ears sit high on the head and then flop down to ½ to 1 inch (1.3–2.5 cm) below the jaw. The wool should be slightly coarse, very dense, and equal in length all over the body.

American Sable

Size: 7–10 pounds (3.2–4.5 kg)

Color: Two shades of sepia brown

The American Sable is a medium-length rabbit with a continuous curve to its topline, and depth and width in all body sections. The Sable has a medium-sized, well-shaped head with erect ears. Buck heads should appear masculine; doe heads should appear more refined. The fur should be a soft, dense, fine fur with coarser guard hairs.

By 1982 the American Sable was almost extinct in the United States and at risk of losing ARBA recognition. However, a group of rabbit breeders organized to continue the breed and improve it. They have successfully met the challenge of growing the breed and maintaining ARBA recognition.

Angora

Size: Depends on the variety

Color: Himalayan marked (pointed white), blue-eyed white, ruby-eyed white, agouti, chinchilla, chocolate chinchilla, lilac chinchilla, squirrel, chestnut agouti, chocolate agouti, copper agouti, lynx agouti, opal agouti, broken, black, blue, chocolate, lilac, pearl, sable, seal, smoke pearl, blue tortoiseshell, chocolate tortoiseshell, lilac tortoiseshell, tortoiseshell, blue steel, chocolate steel, lilac steel, steel, cream, fawn, red

The Angora is an ancient breed that has been previously known as the White Shock Turkey Rabbit and the English Silk Rabbit. Although it may have come originally from Turkey, the modern-day Angora more likely came from England. It has been bred in England for over 200 years. The Angora is the only rabbit breed whose hair can be used for spinning. Because of its long coat, the Angora will need frequent brushing and grooming. Angoras should be taught to sit for grooming after they are several weeks old.

The English Angora weighs between 5 and 7 pounds (2.3–3.2 kg) and has long, dense, silky hair. It

The Angora.

should look like a round ball of fur with short fringed and tassled ears. The body is short with a full chest and shoulder to balance the hips. The ears are erect.

The French Angora is larger than the English, weighing between 7½ and 10½ pounds (3.4–4.8 kg). The shoulders should be slightly narrower than the hips to form a taper. The head is oval and balanced with the body that it sits close to. The French usually has more intense coloring than the English.

The Giant Angora is also a large rabbit, weighing 8½ pounds (3.9 kg) and up. The French Angora and Giant Angora are considered commercial-type rabbits with a strong, sturdy frame. The Giant has noticeable head trimmings. The Giant's wool has three hair types. Most of the hair is the soft, medium-fine underwool. The awn or guard hair is strong, straight hair poking through the fleece. The awn fluff is found between the awn hair and underwool and is a strong, wavy wool with a guard hair tip.

The Satin Angora weighs between 6½ and 9½ pounds (3–4.3 kg). Its wool is finer than the wool of other Angora breeds and generally has a more brilliant color. The Satin has a medium-length body with a slight taper from the hind end to the shoulders. The head is oval, balanced to the body, and has some side trimmings.

Argentes

Size: 5–8 pounds (2.3–3.6 kg)
Color: Black, blue, brown, or creamy white with silvering

The Argente Champagne is considered the oldest fur breed in the world. The Argente has been raised in France for its fur for three centuries. There are four varieties, each defined by its fur color: the Champagne, the Bleu, the Brun, and the Crème. The Argente Crème is the smallest of the group; the Argente Champagne is the largest. It is not registered with the ARBA.

Belgian Hare

Size: 6–9½ pounds (2.7–4.3 kg)
Color: Deep red of a tan or chestnut shade with a slate blue undercolor

The Belgian Hare is long and narrow with a classic hare appearance. Despite its name, it is indeed a rabbit and not a hare. The flanks and ribs are well tucked up and the body is lean. The erect ears are thin and fine. The head sits on a slender neck and is narrow. The fur tends to be stiff and close and the Belgian Hare has a slightly longer tail than most rabbits have.

This breed did not originate from the hare; it originated in England and Belgium. In England, the Belgian Hare was bred in the late 1800s from meat rabbits. This is a popular European breed.

Beveren or Van Beveren

Size: 8–12 pounds (3.6–5.5 kg)
Color: Black, blue, white

A Belgian hare.

This Belgian breed originated in the late 1800s, most likely from crossing the St. Nicholas Giant and the Vienna Blue. The Beveren was one of the first fur breeds and was considered a mainstay of the early fur industry. Its coat is very silky. In the twentieth century, this breed became popular in England and France.

The Beveren has two characteristic facial features: a curve from the forehead to the top of the nose, and long broad ears held in the shape of a V. Although I have never met a Van Beveren, I understand that they are not good with children. This breed is not recognized by the ARBA.

Britannia Petite

Size: Under 2½ pounds (1.1 kg)

Color: Ruby-eyed white, black otter, black, chestnut agouti

The Britannia Petite also has many harelike characteristics. This rabbit has a slender, fine-boned body with a full arch and tucked belly. The head should be wedge-shaped and broad across the forehead. The neck is short. The erect ears are in contact with each other for their full length. The Britannia's fur is sleek and silky.

Californian

Size: 8–10 pounds (3.6–4.5 kg)

Color: White with near black nose, ears, feet, and tail

In 1923 this breed was created in California by crossings that included Chinchillas, Himalayans, and New Zealand Whites. The goal was to produce a rapidly maturing meat breed of rabbit.

The Californian is a medium-sized rabbit with short legs. It should be well developed with firm flesh. The erect ears are proportionate to the size of the body. The shoulders should be slightly lower than the hips with an overall plump body structure.

Champagne d'Argent

Size: 9–12 pounds (4.1–5.5 kg)

Color: Bluish white interspersed with jet black hairs and with a dark slate blue undercolor

There is evidence of this breed from as early as 1631. The Champagne has characteristics of a meat breed rabbit. It is well developed throughout its body, plump, and with firm flesh. The erect ears are well furred and proportionate to the body. The Champagne's head is well shaped and set close to the body. The body rises up from lower-set shoulders to form a curve reaching its highest point over the hips.

The nose and muzzle have a darker color than the body that forms a butterfly. This pattern is one of the distinct characteristics of this breed. All Champagnes are born black and begin to show white hairs at about two months of age.

Checkered Giant

Size: Adults weigh over 11 pounds (5 kg)

Color: White with black or blue markings

The Checkered Giant has a body shape that is more typical of a hare than a rabbit. It is long and well arched so that the belly does not rest on the floor. Buck heads tend to be larger than doe heads and the heavy-set ears are carried both erect and close together.

As the name implies, the Checkered Giant has markings. The short, dense fur is primarily white with black or blue markings. There is a line of color from the ear base to the

A close-up of a Californian rabbit.

tip of the tail, referred to as the spine marking. The side markings consist of two spots on each side, or two groups of spots. The head is heavily marked. The ears are fully covered, the eyes are circled, and cheek spots are present on each side. There is also a butterfly marking on the nose and lips. Markings in other areas are considered undesirable.

Chinchilla

Size: 5½–6¾ pounds (2.5–3.1 kg)
Color: Chinchilla

The Chinchilla is a fine-boned rabbit bred in 1913 by a French engineer who crossed a wild rabbit, a blue Van Beveren, and a Himalayan. This breed arrived in America in 1919, but it is not recognized by the ARBA; the ARBA recognizes larger chinchilla rabbits. Its fur is very similar to that of the wild chinchilla of South America.

The original strains of Chinchilla rabbit had varied genetic patterns. As a result, when they were bred, they did not always produce more of the Chinchilla breed. Different breeds were mixed with these early Chinchilla rabbits to stabilize the gene pool and create greater consistency. Due to the mixing of different breeds, there are some recessive traits that show up that are traits of other breeds. For example, some Chinchillas showing a recessive gene pattern will be "woolies" with a different coat as a result of the breed having been mixed with Angoras.

Cinnamon

Size: 8½–11 pounds (3.9–5 kg)
Color: Rust or cinnamon color with gray ticking on the back and gray color on the sides and belly

The Cinnamon has a typical rabbit shape with a curve up to the hips, which are deeper and wider than the shoulders. The head is proportionate to the body and has erect ears. The Cinnamon has characteristic markings. There are two rust-colored spots inside the hind legs. There is a distinct mask or butterfly effect on the nose, and small eye circles are present.

Crème d'Argent

Size: 8–11 pounds (3.6–5 kg)
Color: Creamy white with a bright orange undercoat

The Crème d'Argent is a medium-length rabbit with an arched back. Although the shoulders and hips are both well developed, the shoulders are slightly narrower so that the body tapers gently to the front. The head, which is more developed in bucks than does, is carried erect and close to the body. The erect ears have a strong base and rounded tips.

The entire body from head to tail should be the same color, creamy white with orange guard hairs and a bright orange undercolor. The belly, however, is creamy white without orange guard hairs. The nose and muzzle should display the butterfly marking that is characteristic of the breed. As with many rabbit breeds, the colors tend to fade in older rabbits.

Deilenaar

Size: 5½–8 pounds (2.5–3.6 kg)

The Deilenaar is a young Dutch breed that is not yet recognized by the ARBA. It was bred in the first half of the twentieth century and introduced to the United States in the 1970s. The Deilenaar is a cross from the Belgian Hare, the New Zealand Red, and the Chinchilla.

Dutch

Size: 3½–5½ pounds (1.6–2.5 kg)

Colors: White with black, blue, brown gray, chocolate, steel, or tortoise

This adorable little rabbit is perhaps best identified by its marking pattern. The Dutch is white on the front of its face, the front part of its body, and its rear paws. Its body is colored from the saddle line to the tail and down the hind legs to the foot stops, where the foot becomes white. The belly is also colored from what is called the undercut line to the back and down the legs. The cheeks and ears have continuous color as well. The markings and their position are the most important factors in judging the Dutch. The erect ears are stocky and well furred.

The fur of the Dutch is dense and short with a high luster. The coarse guard hairs should resist the hair being stroked forward to the head. The coat should also fly back to its natural position. In the Dutch, the steel color is not gray but black with off-white color on some of the hair tips.

Dwarf Hotot

Size: Under 3 pounds (1.4 kg); ideal is 2½ pounds (1.1 kg)

Color: White

The Dwarf Hotot is a tiny, compact rabbit that looks like someone sent it to the makeup department. It is pure white except for rich, dark black eyebands completely outlining the eye. The body is well rounded and uniformly wide from the shoulders to the hips. The head is bold with good width between the eyes. An ideal length for the short ears is 2¼ inches (5.7 cm).

English Lop

Size: 9 pounds (4.1 kg) and over

Color: Agouti group, broken group, self group, shaded group, ticked group, wide band group

The ears of the English Lop are so prominent and so long that a yardstick is often used to measure them. They are measured from the tip of one ear to the tip of the other ear and should measure 21 inches (53 cm) or more. These prominent ears lie down the side of the head— therefore, the lop designation. Ear growth is considered complete at four months of age.

In profile, the English Lop is mandolin-shaped. The shoulders, midsection, and hindquarters are all well developed. A dewlap is permissible in both bucks and does.

In the early English breeding programs, the Lop was considered delicate and therefore was raised in heated housing. Over time, the breed was weakened but a hardy form was then developed that can be kept and bred outdoors.

English Spot

Size: 5–8 pounds (2.3–3.6 kg)

Color: White with black, blue, chocolate, gold, gray, lilac, tortoise

The English Spot is another breed of rabbit that has a harelike appearance. It was bred in England by mixing the Flemish Giant, English Lop, Angora, Dutch, Silver, and Himalayan.

A French Lop with her babies.

The body is balanced and long to show a full arch, leaving the body carried well off the ground. The Spot's coat should appear smooth and should fly back. The fur has many short guard hairs that add luster.

As the name implies, this is a spotted rabbit and should have distinct, clean markings without color running into the white fur. There is a butterfly marking across the nose and lips, and circles around the eyes. Below the eye, and separate from the eye circles, should be a round spot of color on each cheek. The ears are completely colored. A herringbone pattern should be present on the edges of the spine marking. Finally, there are notable side markings. There is a chain of colored spots from the neck down the body and groups of markings along the body and hips. The side patterns should be exactly alike on each side.

Flemish Giant or Patagonian

Size: 13 pounds (5.9 kg) and over
Color: Black, blue, fawn, light gray, sandy, steel gray, white

Not just a big rabbit—a really big rabbit. This breed originated in Belgium, perhaps near Ghent. The Flemish Giant should be very long and large, but well balanced and not fat. The ear base is an important feature in this rabbit and should be heavy and full at the base of the erect ear. Six inches (15 cm) or more is an ideal length for the ear. Does may have a large, full dewlap.

Florida White

Size: 4–6 pounds (1.8–2.7 kg)
Color: Pure white

The Florida White is a small white rabbit that appears rounded since the depth of the body is about the same as the width. The topline curves up from the base of the ears to the center of the hips and then curves down to the tail. Ears are erect, stocky, and well furred.

The Florida White, as the name indicates, was developed in Florida and is a good meat rabbit. It was produced by crossings of Dutch and Polish rabbits, then matched with the New Zealand White.

French Lop

Size: 10 pounds (4.5 kg) and over
Color: Agouti group, broken group, self group, shaded group, ticked group, wide band group

The French Lop is a massive, heavily muscled rabbit. The hindquarters should be deeper and heavier than the shoulders. Only does may have a dewlap to meet breed regulations. A Lop's head is strong and wide. The ears rise from a strong crown and fall to the sides of the head. The ears of the French Lop are in proportion to its body, normally extending 1½ inches (3.8 cm) or more past the jaw.

Giant Chinchilla

Size: 12–16 pounds (5.5–7.3 kg)
Color: Chinchilla

The Giant Chinchilla is known in Europe as the Chinchilla Giganta. It was developed after World War I in both England and Germany under separate breeding programs. The goal of the breeding programs was to develop a large rabbit with both a good pelt and good meat. It is officially recorded as having originated in France, as is the Chinchilla.

The Giant Chinchilla is, of course, a big rabbit. The body is not only long but massive and powerful. It is relatively heavy boned with a well-rounded rump. The back rises and arches. Does may have a dewlap. The erect ears have a stocky base and a jet black color at the upper edges.

Giant Papillon

Size: 13–14 pounds (5.9–6.4 kg)
Color: White with markings

The Giant Papillon is a European breed that is not recognized by the ARBA in the United States. It is a large French version of the English Spot. Instead of a chain of spots on the flanks like the English Spot, the Giant Papillon has patches on its flanks. The other markings are the same.

Harlequin

Size: 6½–9½ pounds (3–4.3 kg)
Color: Black, blue, chocolate, lilac

The Harlequin is a medium-sized rabbit that carries its erect ears in a V. Its most distinguishing feature is its beautiful markings. In the Japanese varieties, the fur is patterned with one of the four colors listed and golden orange or fawn. In the Magpie varieties, the color is mixed among white sections.

Ideally, the face is split in half with color, for example, white on one half and blue down the other half. The ear should be colored with the opposing color so that the white half of the face would have a blue ear in the above example. The pattern over the back may be banded or barred or both, so long as the lines are clean and distinct and colors alternate. Ideally, there will be five to seven alterations of bands and/or bars on each side of the body. Legs should alternate color as well, for example, right front and left back leg white with a left front and right rear leg of blue.

Harlequin patterns are seen in other animals as well; the Great Dane breed of dog, for example, can be harlequin in color. The Harlequin rabbit originated in France.

Havana

Size: 4½–6½ pounds (2–3 kg)
Color: Black, blue, chocolate

The Havana breed began in the Netherlands in 1898, showing a color that had not been seen before. The original breed was crossed with Himalayans to fix the new factor that produced this unusual color. It was after these breedings that the rabbits became known as Havanas. A similar rabbit was shown in 1902 at the Paris Exhibition. The Havana has given rise to several other European rabbit breeds including the Feh de Marbourg, the Perlefee, and the Gris Perle de Hal.

The Havana rabbit should have the same color from tip to tail. It is a short and compact yet well-rounded rabbit. The head should appear to be joined directly to the shoulders rather than to be sitting on the neck. Ears are carried erect and close together.

Himalayan

Size: 2½–4½ pounds (1.1–2 kg)
Color: Black, blue, chocolate, lilac

No, we have not confused our rabbits with our cats; however, the Himalayan rabbit does have color patterns similar to the Himalayan cat. The majority of the rabbit is pure white. The markings on the nose, ears, tail, feet, and legs will be black, blue, chocolate, or lilac. The extremities develop these colors because those areas are colder than the core body. This process takes time; the rabbits are born without these markings. Because the darker color is temperature-regulated, if very young Himalayans are subjected to the cold, more of the body will be colored rather than white.

The body of the Himalayan is quite long and narrow, giving it a cylindrical or tubular appearance. The top and side lines are straight rather than curved. Ears are erect and thin with a taper at the tip. A Himalayan's fur is short and silky and does have flyback properties.

No single country is given credit for the development of this breed. In Europe, the Himalayan was also known as the Russian and the Chinese. This rabbit is considered quite docile and, therefore, an excellent pet.

An all-white Holland Lop taking a snooze.

Holland Lop

Size: Under 4 pounds (1.8 kg)

Color: Agouti group, broken group, pointed white group, self group, shaded group, ticked group, wide band group

Despite its small size, the Holland Lop is thickset and well muscled. It is not quite the delicate little rabbit you might expect. The shoulders are almost as wide as the hindquarters. The head should appear massive and in proportion to the body. Because the head is held high, the lop ears do not fall to the ground. Ears should extend no more than one inch (2.5 cm) below the jaw line. The Holland Lop has a strongly defined crown ridge of cartilage and dense fur.

Hotot

Size: 8–11 pounds (3.6–5 kg)
Color: White

The Hotot is a larger version of the Dwarf Hotot. Just like the Dwarf, the Hotot is a white rabbit with distinctive black rings fully encircling its eyes. The Hotot has a thickset, well-rounded body. Females may have a dewlap. Ears are well furred and carried in a V.

The fur is fine but dense with an abundance of guard hairs. The guard hairs create a frosty sheen that is characteristic of this breed. Ideally, the fur is 1¼ inches (3.2 cm) in length.

Jersey Wooly

Size: Under 3½ pounds (1.6 kg)

Color: Chestnut agouti, chinchilla agouti, opal agouti, squirrel agouti, pointed white with black, pointed white with blue, black, blue, chocolate, lilac, blue-eyed white, ruby-eyed white, shaded blue tortoiseshell, shaded sable point, shaded seal, shaded siamese sable, shaded smoke pearl, shaded tortoiseshell, tan pattern black otter, tan pattern blue otter, tan pattern sable marten, tan pattern silver marten (black, blue, chocolate, lilac), tan pattern smoke pearl marten

The Jersey Wooly is a small rabbit with a lot of hair. The wool has a predominance of guard hairs over crimped underwool. That makes it an easy-to-care-for coat with a healthy luster despite its coarse texture. Ideally, the wool is 2 to 3 inches (5.1–7.6 cm) in length and uniform over the body. Color may appear lighter on the head, ears, and feet. The Jersey Wooly has small, erect, well-furred ears. There are side trimmings on the head of longer fur along the jawline and a wool cap of short wool from the ears forward.

Lilac

Size: 5½–8 pounds (2.5–3.6 kg)

Color: Lilac

This docile breed was developed in different places throughout Europe at different times. Credit for the first breeding is given to a Cambridge, England, citizen who produced the Lilac in 1910. Because the breed was developed in different places at the same time, it originally had different names at different locations. These names included the Essex Lavender, the Cambridge Blue, the Gouda, the Marburger or Marbourg, and the Gouwenaar.

The Lilac has a well-filled compact body that tapers from the hips to the shoulders. Its fur is dense and soft to the touch. The fur should resist stroking against it and maintain a well-groomed appearance.

Lotharinger

Size: 11 pounds (5 kg)

Color: White with black markings

This European breed is not recognized by the ARBA. The Lotharinger is a large breed with the body of a Flemish Giant and a coat similar to the Rhinelander. The body is white. Black coloring appears as a butterfly marking on the nose, on the eye circles, cheek spots, and colored ears, and as spots on the flanks.

Mini Lop

Size: 4½–6½ pounds (2–3 kg)

Color: Agouti group, broken group, pointed white group, self group, shaded group, ticked group, wide band group

An otter-colored Netherland Dwarf (center) and some little friends.

Despite its name, the Mini Lop is not the smallest of the lop rabbits; the Holland is. Like the other lops, the Mini is heavily muscled and compact. Shoulders are broad and deep and rise to slightly heavier hindquarters. The ears are well placed on top of the head and fall close to the cheeks. Like many lop breeds, the outline of the crown and ears is said to form a horseshoe shape. Does may have a dewlap. A Mini Lop's coat should be dense and lustrous with a good rollback.

Mini Rex

Size: 3–4½ pounds (1.4–2 kg)

Color: Black, blue, broken group, castor, chinchilla, chocolate, himalayan, lilac, lynx, opal, red, seal tortoise, white

The Mini Rex is a well-balanced, well-proportioned rabbit. Its compact body has good depth to balance its width. The shoulder area, midsection, and hindquarters are all well developed. The shoulders are slightly narrower than the hindquarters, creating a mild taper. The head is slightly more refined in does than bucks. Does are permitted to have dewlaps in show competitions. The erect ears are carried close together.

The fur should be similar to that of the larger Rex rabbit. An ideal fur length is ⅝ inch (1.6 cm) and it should be dense and upright. There should be distinct springy resistance when you touch the coat.

Netherland Dwarf

Size: Under 2½ pounds (1.1 kg)

Color: Self group, shaded group, agouti group, tan pattern group, fawn, himalayan, orange, steel, tortoiseshell

This petite rabbit has ears that seem short even for its small body. The Netherland Dwarf should be compact with shoulders as wide as the hindquarters. The head is round and high set. Ears are erect, well furred and, ideally, 2 inches (5.1 cm) long. The Netherland Dwarf is one of the most popular of the fancy breeds. It has been known to have a higher than average incidence of malocclusion.

New Zealand

Size: 9–12 pounds (4.1–5.5 kg)

Color: Black, red, white

The New Zealand is a meat breed of rabbit and is therefore evaluated primarily on its body condition. It should have a well-filled loin and well-developed hips with shoulders that balance the rest of the body. Although medium in length, the New Zealand has depth, giving it a slightly rounded appearance. The head is

more massive in bucks than in does. Does may have a small dewlap. Ears have a heavy ear base, are carried erect, and are rounded at the tips. All varieties of the New Zealand breed originated in the United States.

Palomino

Size: Under 9½ pounds (4.3 kg)

Color: Golden, lynx

Palomino, as with the horse, defines a color as much as a breed. The Palomino rabbit is a classic-looking rabbit. It was developed in the United States, in Washington State. The Palomino is a medium-length rabbit with well-developed shoulders and hindquarters. The top line arcs smoothly. The head sits close to the shoulder and the ears are carried erect and together. Hair should fly back.

Polish

Size: Under 3½ pounds (1.6 kg)

Color: Black, blue, chocolate, blue-eyed white, ruby-eyed white

Due to its small size and short ears, the Polish rabbit might be confused with the Netherland Dwarf. One difference is that the Polish head is not round, but full, short, and with a slight curve. The body of the Polish has well-rounded hips that are wider than the shoulders. The ears should touch each other all the way up.

The Polish breed originated in England and was exhibited there as early as 1884. Several years later, the breed was exported to Germany where it enjoyed a period of popularity. German breeders are likely responsible for the form of the Polish that we know today.

Rex

Size: 7½–10½ pounds (3.4–4.8 kg)
Color: Black, black otter, blue, broken group, californian, castor, chinchilla, chocolate, lilac, lynx, opal, red, sable, seal, white

The Rex is a rabbit with characteristics of meat producers. It is a well-balanced medium-sized rabbit that is well developed in its loins and hips. The shoulders are slightly narrower and lower than the hips. The head should be in proportion to the body and harmonize with the body. The erect ears are thick and balance with the rest of the body. Rex rabbits should not appear racy.

There are very specific standards set for the fur of the Rex. It is to be at least ½ inch (1.3 cm) long but not longer than ⅞ inch (2.2 cm). The fur should be straight and lustrous. Many guard hairs are present and the coat has a plush, springy feel.

The Rex might be used as an example of how rabbits—or any animal—should *not* be bred. In 1919 a Frenchman found a young rabbit with hardly any fur and then located another. He paired a brother and sister to fix the presumably recessive gene, causing the shorter hair coat. In 1924 the rabbits were shown and became a sensation. Because a lot of money was to be made by breeding them, they were overbred without respect to their health or vitality. Fortunately, today the breed is healthy and vital.

Rhinelander

Size: 6½–10 pounds (3–4.5 kg)
Color: White with black and bright golden orange markings

This is a German breed that includes the English Butterfly breed in its heritage. The Rhinelander rabbit stands more upright rather than low to the ground. It should be long enough to show a graceful arch without the appearance of heaviness in the shoulder or hindquarters. The Rhinelander should appear alert. Its well-furred ears are carried in a V shape.

Fur and markings are important considerations with the Rhinelander. Its fine, dense fur should fly back. Both the black and orange colors should be evenly distributed in the markings—this is considered an essential characteristic. There is a set of six to eight 1-inch (2.5-cm) round markings on each side, on the back part of the body. The Rhinelander also has a butterfly marking and a spine marking. In addition to the butterfly on the nose, the face has round cheek spots and eye circles, and the ears are colored.

Sallander

Size: 6–10 pounds (2.7–4.5 kg)
Color: Pearl

The Sallander is a Dutch breed that is not recognized by the ARBA in the United States. It was first officially recognized in Holland in 1975 and is not well known in any other country. The Sallander is a thickset rabbit similar to the Thuringer, from which it was developed.

Satin

Size: 8½–11 pounds (3.9–5 kg)

Color: Black, blue, broken group, californian, chinchilla, chocolate, copper, red, siamese, white

The Satin breed started in the 1930s in the United States as the result of a defect in a litter of Havana rabbits. Satin fur has a smaller diameter hair shaft than that of other rabbits and has a more transparent hair shell. As a consequence, the pigment shines through the hair more, making the Satin seem to have especially brilliant hair color. Satin fur is dense and silky. The ideal length is 1–1⅛ inch (2.5–2.9 cm).

The Satin has a medium-length body with a continuous curving topline. The topline rises from the ear base, reaches its maximum point over the center of the hips, and falls smoothly toward the base of the tail. The erect ears are well furred.

Silver

Size: 4–7 pounds (1.8–3.2 kg)

Color: Black, brown, fawn with silver/white guard hairs

The Silver has a standard rabbit body shape with a slight taper from the hindquarters to the shoulders and a gradually curving topline. The head is carried high on the shoulders and the ears are straight and erect. Fur and its color are important considerations when evaluating the Silver. The white/silver guard hairs should be evenly distributed and show well against the coat color. The coat should have a snappy flyback.

A black Silver Marten.

Silver Fox

Size: 9–12 pounds (4.1–5.5 kg)

Color: Jet black with silvering

The Silver Fox has a similar body shape to the Silver but is larger and the head does not sit as high on the shoulders. The depth and width of the medium-sized body should be approximately the same. The head is full but not blocky and sits on a compact neck.

Unlike the Silver, the coat of the Silver Fox does not fly back. It remains upright when stroked forward. Ideally, the coat is 1½ inches (3.8 cm) long, dense, and lustrous. The relatively long coat should be evenly silvered over the entire rabbit. Although breeding true color patterns is difficult, the breed has dedicated followers in the United States and Germany.

Silver Marten

Size: 6–9½ pounds (2.7–4.3 kg)

Color: Black, blue, chocolate, sable with silver-tipped guard hairs

This pretty rabbit is of medium length with well-developed shoulders and hindquarters. The head and ears are in proportion to the rest of the body and sit low on a short neck. The fur should fly back and be evenly interspersed with the silver guard hairs. The neck has a silver triangle at the nape that connects by a narrow silver band to the silver white under the jaw. Eye circles, nostrils, and belly will also be silver white in color.

The Silver Marten derives from the Marten that comes in standard marten color and dark marten color.

The marten color is a dark brown. Only a dark marten and an albino will produce 100 percent standard marten rabbits. Two standard color martens will produce 25 percent albinos, 50 percent standard, and 25 percent dark martens.

Standard Chinchilla

Size: 5–7½ pounds (2.3–3.4 kg)
Color: Chinchilla

The Standard Chinchilla is a more compact chinchilla rabbit. It appears almost round since it is about as deep as it is wide. The body is balanced evenly from the shoulders through the hips. The neck is very short. Like the Giant Chinchilla, the erect ears will have black edges on their upper margins. Ideally, the fur is 1¼ inches (3.2 cm) long. The top of the tail is black; the bottom is white.

Tan

Size: 4–6 pounds (1.8–2.7 kg)
Color: Black, blue, chocolate, or lilac with tan

The Tan is a balanced rabbit with longer front legs so that it sits upright rather than low to the ground. It has a different body structure than other breeds of rabbit. Although it has firm muscle tone, it is not bulky. The back curves gently down from the neck to the tail. The head sits high on the neck and carries alert erect ears.

Tan fur is especially glossy and polished. The short, medium-fine coat has a quick flyback. The tan areas are all the same shade of rich, deep red. The tan color should be seen in eye circles, nostrils, jowls, ears, backs of legs, toes, chest, belly, and tail. The color is also seen as a neck collar that extends to a triangle that reaches the ears. Long tan-tipped guard hairs are seen on the sides and at the rump.

Thuringer

Size: About 8 pounds (3.6 kg)
Color: Light reddish yellow

The Thuringer is a German breed that is not recognized by the ARBA. It came about by crosses of Flemish Giants, Silvers, and Himalayans. In France, the Thuringer is commonly called the Chamois de Thuringe because its color is the same as the Chamois antelope of the Alps.

Viennese

Size: 9 pounds (4.1 kg)
Color: Blue, gray, black, brown

This is another European breed that is not recognized by the ARBA. It is a medium-sized breed that was developed in 1893 in Austria. It is a long rabbit with well-developed shoulders and hindquarters. The coat is very dense. Today, the Viennese is popular in many European countries.

Chapter Ten
Loss of a Pet Rabbit

Whether your rabbit lives 5 years or 12, it is very difficult to lose a beloved pet. In some cases, you will have advanced warning that your pet is in trouble—signs of illness or advanced age. Illness in some rabbits comes on so quickly that you do not even have time to adjust to the fact that they are ill before they are gone. Fortunately, it is now rare for pet rabbit owners to have to deal with the horrible and traumatic death caused by a predator attacking their rabbit.

However old your rabbit is, and whatever the cause of death, it is normal to be upset at the passing of your pet. Although I have seen some people immediately place the death in the normal circle of life and move past it quickly, most people grieve for days or weeks over their loss. The grief may be a simple sadness or a very intense loneliness and loss.

It is sometimes difficult to express or share our grief over the loss of a rabbit. People who do not understand how close a bond can be with a rabbit will not be sympathetic. "It's a rabbit, after all. Can't you just buy another one for $20?" Rabbit, cat, dog, horse . . . what matters is that it was a living being we cared about. We miss cuddly time. We miss feeding time. We miss how the rabbit used to talk to us. We miss that funny way he raced around the couch. We miss him.

Grieving

People handle their grief in many ways. Men often find it easier to deal with it on a personal level, while women tend to find it helpful to have someone to share their sadness with. Children are angry and sad. Young children may not fully understand what has happened. Whatever way you need to grieve for your pet is okay. There is no way that is best or most appropriate.

If you are finding it difficult to sort through your feelings about the loss of your rabbit, there are people to help. Your veterinarian or the staff at the veterinary hospital can provide a comforting ear. Many communities have pet loss support groups for people having a difficult time with

This lazy bunch is a rabbit lover's dream.

the loss of a pet. Even if you just need someone to talk to, you can call one of the national pet loss support hotlines offered by veterinary schools.

Pet Loss Support Hotlines

Chicago Veterinary Medical
  Association
630-603-3994

Cornell University
607-253-3932

Iowa State University
888-478-7574

Michigan State University
517-432-2696

The Ohio State University
614-292-1823

Tufts University
508-839-7966

University of California-Davis
530-752-4200

University of Florida
904-392-4700, then dial 1 and 4080

Virginia-Maryland Regional College
  of Veterinary Medicine
540-231-8038

There can be many feelings to work through during the grieving process. There is not only sadness over the loss but dealing with how the loss occurred. Some owners may feel that they did not do enough. "Maybe I should have seen that he was ill sooner. . . ." "Maybe there was something more the

veterinarian could have done. . . ."
"Maybe I wasn't feeding him right. . . ."
Do not beat yourself up over the maybes. The sad truth is that all pets die, no matter how much we love them and how well they are cared for.

Euthanasia

Grieving may become more complicated if you had to make the difficult choice to put your rabbit down, to have him euthanized. None of us wants to be placed in the position of playing God, so to speak, but we also do not want to watch our terminally ill pet die a slow, horrid, painful death. If your rabbit is suffering tremendously, euthanizing him is the last gift you can give him. Euthanasia, performed by a skilled veterinarian, is a peaceful end to life. It is a choice made by a loving owner to prevent suffering. Your veterinarian can help you decide when this option is necessary for your pet and when the right time is. Once you have made the decision to have this done for your rabbit, be comforted in the knowledge that you allowed your rabbit to die a graceful, peaceful death. Know that you did not allow your rabbit to suffer needlessly.

A Practical Note

One hates to bring it up, but there are practical considerations when your pet dies. Not only are you dealing with all the emotional aspects, but you do have to consider what to do with the remains. Some people choose to bury their pet on their property. Some towns and cities have health restrictions that preclude burying pets. You may want to check with your town or city hall. If there are no such limits, it is best to place the remains of your pet in a plastic bag and then in a box or something similar. Bury your pet several feet down. If you do not take these precautions, you run the risk of an errant dog or wild animal digging up the burial site. Before you choose home burial, you should also consider how long you are likely to be living at this home. If it might be a short time, home burial is not the best option.

If you choose not to bury your pet on your own property, another option is to make arrangements with your veterinarian. If your pet dies while the hospital is closed, you should simply place the body in a cold place until it is open. Your veterinarian can arrange for burial, cremation, or a cremation where the ashes are returned to you. The services your veterinarian offers may differ slightly. Having the ashes returned to you after a cremation is the most expensive option. All veterinarians perform these services on-site or contract with a reputable company to perform them. Nothing will happen with your pet's remains that you have not authorized.

Glossary

abdomen: The belly; the area of the body from the diaphragm to the pelvis that holds (primarily) the digestive and urinary tracts

abscesses: Pockets of infection

albino: All-white; an all-white rabbit with pink eyes

anterior: Front end

arch: An arch of the back; an upward curvature of the spine

awn fluff: The soft, crimped wool fibers that end in a straight tip on a Giant Angora rabbit

awn hair: The strong, straight guard hairs of the Giant Angora rabbit

banding: Different bands of color on a single hair

bangs: The longer wool on the top of the head, in front of the ears in some breeds

barred: Elongated spots

base color: Undercolor or color of fur closest to the skin

bell ears: Large, heavy-tipped ears that fall

belt: The line where the white and colored portions of the body meet

blaze: The wedge-shaped white marking on the head of a Dutch rabbit

blemish: Any defect in the appearance of the rabbit

bloom: The superb finish of a coat in good condition

boots: Colorations on the legs and feet of himalayan-marked rabbits

bowed legs: Legs that curve out in the middle like a bow

breed: A class of rabbits in which the rabbits have similar characteristics and those features are reproducible among members of the class

breeder: Commonly used to mean a person who raises a certain variety of rabbits; can also be used to refer to a rabbit that is being used for breeding/reproduction

breeding certificate: A written certificate from the owner of a breeding buck that states the pedigree of the buck and the date he was bred to a specific doe

brindling: A mix of two colors with no set pattern

broken coat: Exposure of the undercoat due to molting or missing guard hairs

buck: A male rabbit that has not been castrated/neutered

butterfly: A nose marking shaped like a butterfly with the wings extending out over the whisker beds

butting teeth: Malocclusion of the teeth so that the incisors meet perfectly instead of the upper incisors overlapping the lower

cap: A marking in the Checkered Giant; a line where the lower ear color stops and joins the head color

carriage: The way a rabbit poses or carries itself

castration: Removing both testicles from a buck to render him unable to reproduce

Charlie: A rabbit from a marked breed or broken group that has extremely light markings

chest: The front part of the body from the neck to the abdomen

Cheyletiella: A fur mite

chopped: A body type where the back end is not filled out, but falls sharply from the hip to the tail

cobby: Describing a short and stocky body type

coccidia: Intestinal parasites

condition: The overall state of an animal

conjunctivitis: An inflammation of the tissues around the eye

cow hocks: Hocks that turn in toward each other as a cow's hocks do

crimp: Natural waviness in a wool undercoat

crown: A strong ridge on the top of the head that forms the ear base in some lop-eared rabbits; it is composed of cartilage

culling: The process of removing undesirable rabbits from the litter and keeping only the best rabbits

density: The number of hairs in a given area of skin

doe: A female rabbit

dewclaw: An extra toe on the inside of the front legs that serves no function

dewlap: An extra roll of skin and fur under the chin sometimes seen in does

disqualification: When a rabbit is ineligible for competition because it has a certain defect(s)

drags: Color markings invading a white area

ear lacing: An outline of color on the sides and tips of the ears

Encephalitozoon: A parasite that can cause disease in the brain

enteritis: An inflammation or infection of the intestines

enterotoxemia: A severe form of enteritits

eye color: The color of the iris of the eye

fault: An imperfection, not so substantial as to disqualify a rabbit for show

feathering: A small drag of color off the top of an eye circle

felting: Interwoven wool fibers

fine coat: Fur that is fine in texture with few or weak guard hairs

flanks: The sides of the rabbit behind the ribs

flat coat: Fur lying more closely to the body than desired

fleece: The wool of the rabbit

fly back: The action of the fur returning to its normal position when it is stroked forward; it "flies back"

foreign color: Any color different from that called for in the standard of perfection for the breed

forequarter: The front part of the body, from the neck to the last rib

fringes: The wool on the ears of some breeds

fryer: Three- to ten-week-old rabbit

furnishings: Tassels, ear fringes, bangs, and head side trimmings that occur in some wooled breeds

gestation: The length of pregnancy, beginning at conception and ending with kindling

guard hair: The longer, coarser hairs that extend from the coat and protect the undercoat

herringbone: The colored spinal stripe seen on the English Spot

hind leg: One of the two back legs

hindquarters: The back portion of the body starting at the last rib and ending at the tail

hocks: The pointed joint closest to the foot on the back leg

humpback: A deformity of the spine causing a bump in the back

inbreeding: Breeding closely related rabbits together

intact: Commonly used to refer to the fact that the reproductive organs of a doe or buck have not been removed

junior: A rabbit under six months old

kindling: The process of a doe giving birth to kits

kit: A baby rabbit

lactate: To produce milk to nurse the kits

linebreeding: An attempt to promote characteristics of related rabbits by breeding distantly related rabbits together, for example, rabbits from the same line

litter: A group of kits from the same doe

loin: The side portion of the rabbit from the last rib to the hip

luster: Brilliance of the fur

maggots: Fly larvae

malocclusion: Improper alignment of the teeth

mandolin: Refers to the body shape of some rabbits; having the appearance of a mandolin instrument that is laid face down

marbling: Mottled eye color

marked: Distinctly placed colors breaking up a white (usually) coat

mask: A color marking the nose and muzzle

mastitis: Inflammation or infection of the mammary glands

meaty: Carrying a good portion of meat or muscle in relation to the size and type of the rabbit

mite: A microscopic spider-like organism that can infest rabbits' ears or fur and be transmitted to other rabbits

molt: The process of shedding fur

muzzle: The nose and lower part of the face

myiasis: Invasion of fly larvae into the skin, also called "warbles"

myxomatosis: A virus transmitted to rabbits by mosquitoes

nest box: A box inside a cage or hutch where a doe kindles and where the kits live for the first three weeks of their life

neutering: Technically, removing the reproductive organs of a male or female; commonly used to refer to the removal of both testicles in a buck

This baby Rex looks like the Easter Bunny himself.

nosefork: The portion of a butterfly marking that forms the body and sits on the nose extending up the face

open coat: A coat that does not fly back; it does not return to its nat-ural position after being stroked toward the head

outbreeding: Breeding unrelated rabbits of the same breed

packed: Compacted wool

paralysis: Inability to move

parasite: Any organism that lives on or within another

Passalurus: The rabbit pinworm

Pasteurella: Bacteria that causes severe infections in rabbits including snuffles and can be transmitted from rabbit to rabbit, especially from a doe to her kits

patch : A small area of fur

pea spots: Two color spots at the inside base of the ear in breeds of rabbit with the tan pattern

pedigree: A chart of the ancestors of a particular rabbit

peg teeth: Two short teeth behind the upper incisors

pelt: Animal hide

pencil line: A raised area of fur under the chin and across the throat

perineum: The area between the anus and the vulva in a female, between the anus and the penis in a male

pigeon breasted: Having a narrow chest

pinched hindquarters: Hindquarters that pinch in toward the tail

plush: Fine, dense, soft fur

pneumonia: Bacterial infection of the lungs

points: The markings of the Californian, Himalayan, or Pointed White

posterior: Back end

potbelly: A distended abdomen

prime line: A line of fur developing down the middle of the back

purebred: A term loosely used for rabbits to indicate that a rabbit is from a line that has met the standards of the breed for several generations

pyometra: Infection of the uterus

rabbitry: A place where rabbits are kept or raised

racy: Appearing trim and active

ringworm: A contagious fungal infection of the skin

roll back: The action of the fur gradually returning to its normal position when stroked forward toward the head

Roman nose: A highly bridged nose

rump: The upper, round portion of the hindquarters

run: A white color invading a colored marked area

saddle: The upper portion of the back

senior: For the purposes of show, a rabbit that is at least six months of age

shadow bars: Weakly colored bars across the legs or feet

sheen: A bright luster to the coat, observed primarily in the Satin breed

shoulder: The area of the body that starts at the neck and stops at the upper joint of the front leg and the last rib

side trimmings: Wool on the side of the head

silvering: A silvery gloss to the fur created by silver-tipped guard hairs throughout the fur

slipped crown: Description of the ear position when it is misplaced in a lop-eared breed due to the crown sitting too far forward or back

slipping coat: Shedding coat

slobbers: Wet fur around the mouth and forelegs caused by excess salivation

smut: Large number of dark guard hairs causing a darkness to the color or a stain found in Himalayans, Californians, and Pointed Whites or a nose marking on a Himalayan

snipey: A long, narrow head

snuffles: A respiratory infection in the nose often caused by Pasteurella

solid: A judging group of solid-colored rabbits

sore hocks: Inflammation of the foot pads

spaying: Removing the ovaries and uterus from a doe so that she cannot reproduce

splayed: Describing a condition in which the legs spread out from the body and do not support the rabbit

spraying: Expressing small amounts of urine for the purpose of marking territory

stifle: The second (middle) joint of the back leg, also called the knee

surface color: The top color of the fur

syphilis: A venereal disease of rabbits

tassels: Longer wool on top of the ears

tattoo: A permanent ear marking to identify the rabbit

ticking: Dispersed guard hairs of a different color than the rest of the fur

tint: A variation in the intensity of a color

trichobezoars: Hairballs

tucked up: Describing a position in which the belly is gathered up close to the back so that an arch forms when a rabbit is sitting

Tyzzer's disease: An infection caused by Clostridium piliforme

undercolor: The color of the fur closest to the skin

undercut: The belly marking of a Dutch rabbit

underwool: Short wool fiber lying at the base of a wool coat

urolithiasis: Stones in the urinary tract, usually in the bladder

variety: A subdivision of a recognized breed

wall eye: Whiteness on the surface of the eye; also known as Moon Eye

warbles: Invasion of fly larvae into the skin, also called myiasis

webbed: Describing Angora wool that is beginning to mat

weaning: The process of transferring kits from nursing on their mothers to solid food

wolf teeth: Long or protruding front teeth as a result of a malocclusion

wry neck: A medical condition, often caused by Pasteurella infection of the middle ear, that causes the rabbit to twist its neck to one side

wry tail: A bent or twisted tail

Appendix

Potentially Toxic Plants

Note: Be sure to keep your rabbit away from these plants, but this list should not be interpreted as including *all* potentially toxic plants.

African evergreen
amaryllis
azalea
belladonna
blue-green algae
Boston ivy
Calla; calla lily
castor bean or castor oil plant
chinaberry
chinese evergreen
chives
dumb cane
elephant's ear
foxglove
garlic
hemlock
holly
hyacinth
iris
jimson weed
kalmia
laburnum
lords and ladies (cuckoo spit)
marijuana

mushrooms
narcissus (ex., Daffodil)
nightshade
onion
peace lily
philodendron
pieris
poinsettia
pothos
precatory bean
purple thorn apple
rhododendron
rhubarb
shamrock
spindleberry
spoon flower
tobacco
tropical cycads
tulip
Virginia creeper
wild calla
wisteria
wooly pod milkweed
yew

Useful Addresses and Literature

The number for the **National Animal Poison Control Center is 800-548-2423.** There is a $45 charge for the service of animal poison control that must be paid at the time of the phone call with a credit card. Or, you can call them at 900-680-0000 and the cost will be charged to your phone bill instead. The cost for the 900 number is currently $20 for the first five minutes and $2.95 for each additional minute. At the time this book is being written, this center employs 11 veterinarians dedicated fully to studying and recording poisons in animals and remedies for their toxic effects. They are the best animal poison database in the country.

Organizations
American Rabbit Breeders
  Association, Inc.
P.O. Box 426
Bloomington, IL 61702
(309) 664-7500
Fax: (309) 664-0941
e-mail: ARBAPOST@aol.com
Internet address: www.arba.net

The House Rabbit Society
1524 Benton Street
Alameda, CA 94501
Internet address: www.rabbit.org

Wildlife Rehabilitators
National Wildlife Rehabilitators'
  Association (NWRA)
14 North 7th Avenue
St. Cloud, MN 56303-4766
(320) 259-4086
Internet address:
  www.nwrawildlife.org
  A listing of local rehabilitators is also available on the Internet at the Wildlife Rehabilitation Information Directory at http://www.cc.ndsu.nodak.edu/instruct/devold/twrid/html/hp.htm#aa

Other Useful Internet Sites
Pet Rescue Warehouse
Internet address:
  homearts.com/depts/pastime/
  shelters/shelters.htm
  Lists local shelters that may have rabbits for adoption

The Pet Rabbit Web
Internet address:
  www.petrabbit.com
    Offers general rabbit information

Net Vet and the Electronic Zoo
Internet address:
  www.avma.org/netvet/
    Resource for medical and general
information on all animals

Rabbit Specialty Clubs
  In addition to the following, each
breed of rabbit has its own club.
Names and addresses are available
through the ARBA.

American Dwarf Hotot Rabbit Club
Bobbi Larimer
68 Clover Court
Granville, OH 43023
(614) 587-2231

American Netherland Dwarf
  Rabbit Club
Shannon Byrom
2725 East Lake Avenue
Watsonville, CA 95076
(408) 763-1553

Californian Rabbit Specialty Club
C. Eunita Boatman
22162 South Hunter Road
Colton, OR 97017
(503) 824-2138

Lop Rabbit Club of America
Jeanne Welch
36179 Cabrillo Drive
Fremont, CA 94536
(510) 793-4977

Mini Lop Rabbit Club of America
Pennie Grotheer
PO Box 17
Pittsburg, KS 66762-0017
(417) 842-3317

National Mini Rex Rabbit Club
Karen Heintz
RR 4 Box 175
Pipestone, MN 56164
(507) 825-3641

Magazines
Domestic Rabbits
(published by the American Rabbit
Breeders Association)
P.O. Box 426
Bloomington, IL 61702

The House Rabbit Journal
(published by the House Rabbit
Society)
1524 Benton Street
Alameda, CA 94501

Rabbits Only
P.O. Box 207
Holbrook, NY 11741
(516) 737-0763
(516) 737-1905
Internet address:
  http://www.rabbits.com

Rabbit Fancy
Available in pet and magazine stores

Index

Abscess, 53
Aggression, 78
Alaska, 102
American, 102
American Checkered Giant, 102
American Chinchilla, 102
American Fuzzy Lop, 103
ARBA/American Rabbit Breeders
    Association, 94, 131
American Sable, 103
Angora, 31, 103–104
Antibiotics, 52, 56
Argentes, 105
Australia, 6

Behavior, 75–79
Belgian Hare, 105
Beveren, 105
Birth, 85–86
Biting, 77–79
Body language, 76–79
Bowls, 24–25
Breeding, 84–87
Britannia Petite, 106
Brushing, 32
Burial, 123

Cage
    Carrying/Travel, 23, 37
    Cleaning, 25
    Construction, 24
    Size, 23
Californian, 106, 107
Champagne d'Argent, 106
Checkered Giant, 106–107
Children, 11–12
Chinchilla, 108
Cinnamon, 108
Coccidia, 53–54
Colors, 98–100
Coprophagy, 41, 79
Crème d'Argent, 108

Death, 120–123
Deilenaar, 108–109
Diarrhea, 54
Digging, 75–76
Dog racing, 3–4
Dogs, 15
Dutch, 109
Dwarf Hotot, 109

Ears, 33, 54
Easter, 3
Electric shock, 22
Encephalitozoon, 55
English Lop, 5, 109
English Spot, 109–110
Enteritis, 55–56
Enterotoxemia, 56–57
Euthanasia, 123
Experiments, 8
Eyes, 2, 50–51, 66

Flemish Giant, 110
Florida White, 97, 111
First aid kit, 48
Fleas, 57
Flies, 62–63, 65
Food, 42–46, 85, 90
Foreign bodies, 57–58
French Lop, 110, 111
Fur production, 8

Genetics, 91–93
Giant Chinchilla, 111
Giant Papillon, 111
Grade rabbit, 13
Grand Champion, 96
Grooming, 30–34

Hairballs, 57–58
Hair loss, 59
Handling, 21–22
Hares, 1

Harlequin, 111–112
Havana, 112
Head tilt, 60
Heatstroke, 28–29, 60
Hepatic lipidosis, 61
Himalayan, 112
Holland Lop, 71, 113
Hotot, 113–114
Hutch, 26–29

Illness, signs of, 49, 89
Introduction, to house, 17
Introduction, to pets, 18–19

Jackalope, 9
Jersey Wooly, 114

Kidney disease, 61
Kindling, 85–86
Kits, 86

Lagamorphs, 1
Lilac, 114
Litter, 30
Litter training, 29
Lops, 5, 13, 71, 94, 103, 109–111, 113–115
Lotharinger, 114

Maggots, 62–63
Malocclusion, 63–64
Marking, 76
Mastitis, 64–65
Meat Rabbit, 8
Medicating Rabbits, 50–52
Microchip, 39
Milkweed, 65
Mini Lop, 114–115
Mini Rex, 115–116
Mites, ear, 54
Mites, fur, 58
Myiasis, 65
Myxomatosis, 6, 66

Nail trim, 34
Nest box, 86

Netherland Dwarf, 115, 116
Neutering, 79, 82–83, 116
Newborns, 87–91
New Zealand (breed), 116
New Zealand (country), 4–5

Orchitis, 67
Orphans, 89–91
Outdoor housing, 26–29

Pain, 49
Palomino, 116
Papillomatosis, 67
Paralysis, 68–69
Pasteurella multocida, 53, 67–68, 69, 70
Pedigree, 13, 95
Pneumonia, 70–71
Poisoning, 22, 49–50, 65, 131, Appendix
Porphyrin pigment, 70
Polish, 116
Pregnancy, 69
Purebreds, 94–96
Pyometra, 69

Red urine, 70
Registration, 94–96
Respiratory disease, 70–71
Rex, 20, 117, 127
Rhinelander, 117
Ringworm, 71–72

Sallander, 117
Satin, 119
Selection
  Age, 15
  Breeds, 13, 100–120
  Male or Female, 15
  Other pets, 18
  Sources, 12
Sexing, 81–82
Sexual maturity, 83
Shows, 96–97
Silver, 119
Silver Fox, 119
Silver Marten, 119–120

Slobbers, 63–64
Snuffles, 67, 71
Sore hocks, 68
Spaying, 16, 79, 82–83
Spinal fractures, 68–69
Standard Chinchilla, 120
Standard of perfection, 94
Syphilis, 72

Tan, 120
Tattoo, 39
Teeth, 63–64
Teeth grinding, 49
Temperature of rabbit, 48, 60
Thuringer, 120
Toys, 25
Travel, 34, 48
Tyzzer's Disease, 72

Urinary incontinence, 72–73
Urolithiasis, 73–74
Uterine adenocarcinoma, 74

Veterinarian, 17, 48
Viennese, 120
Viral hemorrhagic disease,
    74
Voice, 76

Warbles, 65
Warren, 23
Water, 45–46
Weaning, 87
Wild rabbit, 75, 87–89
Wool rabbit, 8
Worms, intestinal, 61
Wry neck, 60